# THE
# AMUNDSEN
## *PHOTOGRAPHS*

# THE AMUNDSEN
## PHOTOGRAPHS

*EDITED AND INTRODUCED*

*BY ROLAND HUNTFORD*

THE ATLANTIC MONTHLY PRESS

NEW YORK

*Also by the same author*

SCOTT AND AMUNDSEN
(The Last Place on Earth)

SHACKLETON

First USA Edition

ISBN 0-87113-171-4

Book designed by Trevor Vincent
Printed in Italy

First Printing

# CONTENTS

NORWEGIAN CURRENCY

The contemporary rate of exchange of the Norwegian krone
was about 18.4 to the pound sterling and 3.75 to the US dollar.
The purchasing power of the krone in 1987 terms
was £1.40 or $2.20.


PUBLISHER'S NOTE

The pictures in this book
are reproduced from Amundsen's glass slides
in the condition in which they were discovered – cracks and all.
There has been no attempt to veil the ravages of time.

# *INTRODUCTION*

In England, late in 1912, a Bristol schoolgirl heard Roald Amundsen lecture on his attainment of the South Pole. "Hardly contain myself all day," she jotted in her diary, although the event itself went back a year to the 14th December 1911. "Amundsen," as she put it, "had a simply killing Norwegian accent. And we had to consentrate [*sic*] for all we were worth to be able to understand what he said." His lantern slides were "mostly coloured and simply *lovely*". Best of all, "Amundsen told us that many people asked what was the use of trying to get to the S. Pole etc. etc. The man said with the *utmost* scorn, 'Little minds have only room for thoughts of bread & butter.'"

Before sound film, video, or television, the lantern lecture was the great means of presentation, the only way of extending the season of profit and acclaim. It was a highly personal medium; each performance was live and *sui generis*.

More than merely the first man at the South Pole, Amundsen was one of those driven souls who have shaped our century. With Grieg and Ibsen, he was one of the celebrated Norwegians who brought their country out of the obscurity of Northern mists. Polar exploration was his ruling passion.

Amundsen once remarked that he was glad that he had not been born later, because then there would have been nothing left for him except to be the first man on the moon. There was something in this. During the last quarter of the nineteenth century, exploration seemed to have lagged behind other fields of human enquiry. When Amundsen was born, the earth had not yet been fully explored. Less was known about the surface of the globe than the bright side of the moon. The polar regions were largely blanks upon the map. Neither North nor South Poles had been reached; nor, for that matter, had the interior of Greenland. Except for part of the coastline, the whole of Antarctica was unknown. The central Arctic basin was still *terra incognita*. Even the waters off Siberia and the Canadian Arctic were imperfectly charted.

To the exclusion of practically all else, Amundsen devoted himself to the probing of these mysteries. For thirty years, he returned again and again to high latitudes. Finally, in June 1928, he disappeared in the Arctic, and

was seen no more. He left his house, on the shore of the Oslo Fjord, exactly as it stood, down to the book he was reading, open at the place where he broke off. His possessions were in disarray. Amongst other things, his lantern slides were thought to have been lost.

In the spring of 1986, an exhibition was organized at Vadsø, in northern Norway, to commemorate the sixtieth anniversary of Amundsen's flight in an airship from Norway to Teller, Alaska, via Spitsbergen and the North Pole – the first flight across the Arctic. Although Amundsen is remembered best as the first man at the South Pole, he was famous in his day for other exploits too.

Seeking new memorabilia, the exhibition organizers approached Mrs Alda Amundsen, the widow of Gustav Amundsen, the explorer's nephew and heir. From the attic of her Oslo flat, Mrs Amundsen produced a likely-looking packing case labelled "Horlicks Malted Milk". She assumed that it contained supplies left over from one of Amundsen's expeditions. When it was opened, in Vadsø, the contents turned out to be more than two hundred of Amundsen's original lantern slides.

For his lectures on the South Pole, Amundsen is known to have had several sets of slides prepared. Hitherto, a few cracked and faded specimens were all that were thought to have survived. The new collection included the first more or less complete set to be recovered. Because of the accident of being "lost" and left undisturbed down the years, it had been preserved in something like its original condition.

When Amundsen departed for the South Pole, photography was of another order than the present day computerized technique. The roll film, as distinct from the photographic plate, was well established but, outside the cinema, the now familiar 35mm format was still experimental. The commonest size was quarter plate, or 4¼" × 3¼", on a film 3½" (8.7cms) wide. The films held between eight and twelve exposures, and were considerably heavier than a modern cassette with thirty-six frames. Cameras were correspondingly bulky and had to be used, preferably, with restraint. One picture, one shot, was the rule.

The transparency, as we know it, did not exist. For projection on a screen special photographic plates were printed from negatives, then bound up together with clear glass plates to protect the emulsion and form the finished, but still fragile lantern slides (usually 3¼" × 3¼"). A lecturer on tour was, therefore, burdened by heavy, awkward, oblong wooden cases holding his precious slides, and having to be handled with the utmost care. The projectors were correspondingly clumsy: large devices, often powered by arc lamps, fixed equipment of the various venues, and notoriously in the hands of incompetent operators.

Among those who also heard Amundsen lecture in England during 1912 was Kathleen Scott, the widow of Captain Scott, whom Amundsen had beaten in the race for the South Pole. She was present at his opening appearance, at the Queen's Hall, London, on the 15th November. Amundsen's pictures, she decided, "were very poor, & many of them faked – painted etc". Those were the days before universal colour photography. Black and white was the rule. Prints and lantern slides, however, were frequently coloured by hand. This held for many of Amundsen's slides. The tints have survived to show what displeased Kathleen Scott, and what delighted that impressionable schoolgirl.

Amundsen was a dedicated professional in most things, but the notable exception was publicity. He was a man of action, with an almost naive faith in his deeds necessarily speaking for themselves. Unlike some of his contemporaries – especially Scott – Amundsen never had a professional photographer on any of his expeditions. He and his companions took pictures themselves as they felt the need. In this alone they were amateurs, and their work was undoubtedly that of the snapshot. Whatever the drawbacks in presentation, this did at least register events as seen through their own eyes. The outcome is a poignant blend of immediacy, artlessness and authenticity. This happens to suit Amundsen's style.

Roald Engelbreth Gravning Amundsen, to give him his full name, was born, the youngest of four brothers, on 16th July 1872, at Borge, near Sarpsborg, on the eastern shore of the Oslo Fjord. His father was a shipowner and merchant skipper; his mother, the daughter of a tax collector. While Roald was still a baby, his family moved up the fjord to Oslo, or Christiania, as the capital of Norway then was known, and there he grew up.

When Amundsen was fourteen years old, his father died. Soon after, by his own account, he decided to become a polar explorer. What is certain is that in 1893 he tried to join, first a projected Norwegian expedition to Spitsbergen, and then an English one to Franz Josef Land under Frederick Jackson. A year later, Amundsen attempted to organize his own expedition to Spitsbergen, and soon afterwards planned a foray to the Antarctic.

None of this came to anything. Amundsen, who had learned to ski as a schoolboy, was already seriously training for polar exploration by going on long ski tours in the Norwegian mountains. Those were still the early days of skiing as a sport, and Amundsen was one of the skiing pioneers. He was known among his friends for his dedication and his profound interest in equipment, at an early age being nicknamed "the Arctic explorer".

Some of those early efforts were as trying and dangerous as anything Amundsen subsequently endured, but they enabled him to make his beginner's mistakes. It soon became Amundsen's intention to avoid the disasters which seemed to be an inescapable consequence of polar exploration.

According to Amundsen himself, he was inspired by the example of two illustrious compatriots. The first was Fridtjof Nansen, the pioneering polar explorer who, in 1888, made the first crossing of Greenland. It was to Eivind Astrup, however, that Amundsen felt most indebted, for Astrup was a somewhat less forbidding figure. Astrup had been with Robert Peary on a celebrated traverse of Northern Greenland in 1891–2; a saga of difficulty, privation, and ultimate triumph. Amundsen heard Astrup lecture on that experience to the Christiania students early in 1893, and that may well have been the impulse that finally sent him on his way.

Meanwhile, Amundsen's family was becoming seriously concerned about his waywardness. To please his mother, Amundsen had begun studying medicine, but he was not academically inclined and, in 1893, he failed his first examinations. The same year, his mother died, he felt absolved from his obligations, and he left university.

The Amundsen family were substantial shipowners and, by Norwegian standards, quite well off. Roald had a reasonable inheritance and, while at university, had lived in style. Nonetheless, it was imperative that he acquire a profession. At the instigation of his elder brother, Gustav, he followed the family tradition, and went to sea.

Even so, Amundsen kept his distant goal in sight. His first ship was an Arctic sealer, *Magdalena*, in which, during 1894, he sailed before the mast, and had his baptism of the polar ice. The sealing itself appalled him and, as he afterwards said, he could "never understand those who killed animals for sport". In May 1895, Amundsen obtained his mate's certificate and, after a second sealing voyage for sea time, qualified as a merchant officer. He had satisfied his family, to a certain extent.

Two years later, Amundsen finally joined his first polar expedition. This was an Antarctic enterprise, led by Baron Adrien de Gerlache, a Belgian, sailing in a converted sealer called *Belgica*. The experience was a nightmare. *Belgica* was caught by the pack ice in the uncharted Bellingshausen Sea, south of Cape Horn, and drifted helpless for a year. Her polyglot company were ill prepared for what they had to face. Insanity and disease stalked the ship.

One of Amundsen's shipmates happened to be Dr Frederick A. Cook, the American who later made what was widely alleged to be a fraudulent claim to have reached the North Pole. But on *Belgica*, Amundsen saw in Cook – who had already been to Greenland with Peary – an accomplished teacher of polar technique, besides being a dedicated physician. Amundsen was convinced that Cook saved the expedition from disaster.

For all its defects, the drift of the *Belgica* was one of the great pioneering polar enterprises. It was the first expedition ever to winter in Antarctica, paving the way for modern Antarctic exploration. On Brabant Island, off the coast of Graham Land, Amundsen actually took part in the first Antarctic sledging journey.

Amundsen was now launched, at last, on his chosen career. Whatever he started, however, he preferred to finish. His service on *Belgica* counted towards qualifying for master. Soon after returning to Norway, in 1899, Amundsen decided to make up the necessary sea time, and joined another ship, a barque called *Oscar*, which belonged to the Amundsen family. She happened to be lying at the Spanish port of Carthagena, so Amundsen, partly for the exercise, and partly the experience, cycled all the way from Christiania, travelling via Paris and Bordeaux where, incidentally, his family had interests in the wine trade. After a transatlantic voyage in *Oscar*, Amundsen finally qualified as a foreign-going skipper. He belonged to a select and disappearing breed, for he had been trained in sail.

In 1903, Amundsen left Norway on the first polar expedition under his own command. He wanted to navigate the North West Passage, the legendary short cut, along the Arctic coast of North America, from the Atlantic to the Pacific. By now, Amundsen had overcome his family's reservations. Henceforth they helped him to make his way. That did not save him from setting off in debt, "a permanent state of affairs," as he once said.

Amundsen did indeed complete the North West Passage. He then led the expedition which brought him victory at the South Pole. In 1918–20 he made a voyage along the coast of Siberia from Norway to the Bering Strait, thereby becoming the second man in recorded history to sail through the North East Passage. This was the other long-sought sea route from the Atlantic to the Pacific. During that voyage, Amundsen intersected his route on the North West Passage, thereby becoming the first, and so far the only, man to have circumnavigated the Arctic.

These three expeditions are all recorded in the lantern slides, although most concern the attainment of the South Pole. A solitary slide commemorates the cruise of the *Belgica*. Amundsen always looked back on that experience with nostalgia. One of his shipmates later said that Amundsen was the "Napoleon of the Polar Regions", and that *Belgica* was his school.

Glory was, however, ill paid. To Amundsen, money meant nothing, except as a means to pursue his vocation; for a vocation is what he truly had. On the North West Passage, he had spent virtually his whole fortune. The rest of his life was a battle with financial difficulties, relieved by bouts of solvency, with his friends and family trying to save him from himself.

On various occasions, notably after the North West Passage, and before he departed for the South Pole, the Norwegian Government gave Amundsen a grant. Nonetheless, he had to try and earn money as best he could. Books and newspaper rights were not enough. Much as he would have liked, Amundsen could not avoid lecturing.

When that schoolgirl saw Amundsen in Bristol, he was on a world tour after winning the race for the South Pole. It was a universal triumph, for the attainment of the South Pole meant the conquest of the last great geographical goal. It was a symbol of the completion of terrestrial discovery and, for all its intrinsic uselessness, it somehow captured the imagination of the world.

In Amundsen's own words, that lecture tour was "not the same as a pleasure trip". It was "a journey full of strain, with profit earned by the sweat of one's brow". In America, he found himself unwillingly in the hands of reception committees, "just as vital to the American," he sardonically remarked, "as water when one washes." Amundsen did not like committees, anywhere, of any kind. Of his American tour, he wrote feelingly that it "lasted half a year, and in that time, I gave about 160 lectures. I was bundled about like any old parcel . . . I had no rest, day or night . . . I was just part of a lecture machine."

It did not end there. Years afterwards, Amundsen was still tramping round the lecture trail, trying to squeeze what he could out of his accomplishments. It was a deadening exercise; raking over the embers of past triumphs. It partly explains the bitterness of Amundsen's later years. Behind a forbidding exterior there hid a sensitive man with an immense capacity for affection. He never married; he ended lonely and unhappy. It was as if he had been called upon to pay the price of achieving all his goals; beware, as Teresa of Avila said, of having your prayers answered.

Amundsen was no prosaic investigator. He was a dreamer and a man of action. He was pre-eminent in a generation that saw the shrinking of the empty spaces on the map. His lantern slides encapsulate the achievements of a remarkable man. They summarize the end of the classic age of terrestrial discovery, when the polar regions were the last great blanks on the surface of the globe, and men moved under their own power, with ski, sleds, and dogs. Afterwards, came the leap into space. It is a new aspect of a famous story.

# I

# *THE NORTH WEST PASSAGE EXPEDITION*

## *1903–1906*

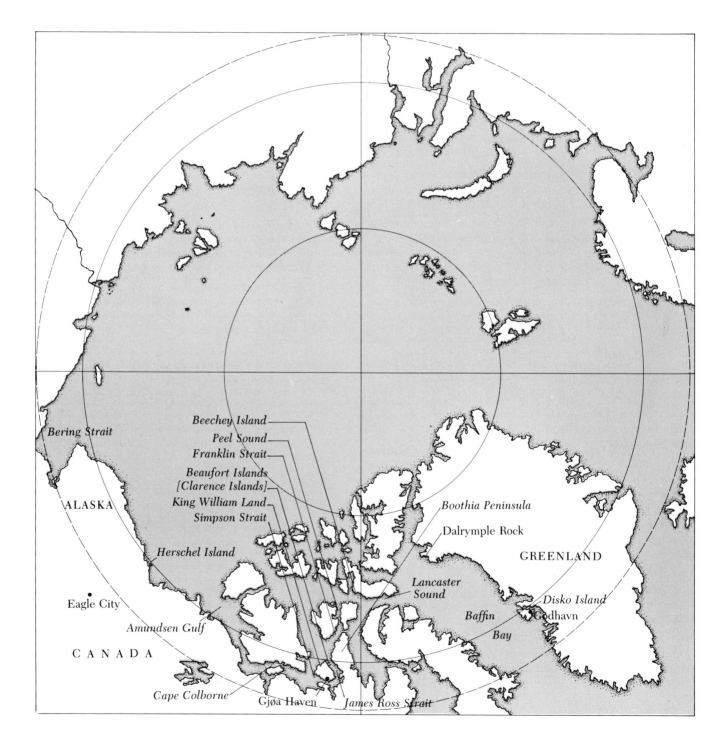

Bering Strait

ALASKA

Herschel Island

Eagle City

Amundsen Gulf

CANADA

Cape Colborne

Gjøa Haven

James Ross Strait

Beechey Island

Peel Sound

Franklin Strait

Beaufort Islands
[Clarence Islands]

King William Land

Simpson Strait

Boothia Peninsula

Dalrymple Rock

GREENLAND

Lancaster
Sound

Disko Island

Godhavn

Baffin

Bay

# THE NORTH WEST PASSAGE EXPEDITION

It was characteristic of Amundsen that he identified with precision the moment when inchoate ambition took concrete form. It was, he always maintained, the 30th May 1889, when Fridtjof Nansen sailed up the fjord and returned home in triumph after the first crossing of Greenland. Amundsen, as he later told the tale, "walked that day among the banners and cheers and all the dreams of my boyhood woke to storming life. And for the first time I heard, in my secret thoughts, the whisper clear and insistent: If *you* could do the North West Passage!"

The North West Passage was a chimera that lured men along the path of exploration. Its beginnings lay in the quest for a seaway to the East; one goal at least of the western European navigators who made the great voyages of discovery during the fifteenth and sixteenth centuries. The caravan routes overland to China were languishing; western Europeans, in the restless, inspiring ambience of the Renaissance, were pushing out into the unknown.

In one quarter, this led to the southern route round the Cape of Good Hope, pioneered by the Portuguese. Westwards, the prospect of a short and simple passage dissolved with the discovery of America, by Christopher Columbus in the service of Spain.

Spain and Portugal quickly monopolized navigation in the southern hemisphere. Trade with the Orient, delicious plunder from the New World, were pouring wealth into the Iberian peninsula. England and France, meanwhile, the rising powers, wanted a share in the eastern trade, and sought a seaway of their own. The shortest way must be northwards, where the meridians converged. Out of this unexceptional theory sprang the belief in a navigable route round the top of North America through an open polar sea. Such was the North West Passage.

From the early sixteenth century, a succession of explorers sought this illusory goal. One was Jacques Cartier, a Breton, who first set sail in 1534, never got anywhere near the Orient, but discovered the St Lawrence River, and founded French Canada. It was a Yorkshireman, Martin Frobisher, who first glimpsed the dismal truth. In 1576, he reached Frobisher Bay in Baffin Island, with its forbidding snow and ice. Thenceforth, the search for a North West Passage became more or less an English

preserve. In the face of setback and disaster, a succession of illustrious navigators were drawn on by the quixotic hope of a passage through a mythical open Arctic sea. In the process, modern polar exploration was born.

By Amundsen's time the North West Passage had long since lost its original significance of a commercial quest for a seaway to the East, acquiring instead the quality of myth. Like the North Pole, and the sources of the Nile, it had become one of the great geographical goals that symbolized the end of the age of discovery. Its achievement had become an end in itself.

The first men to discover a North West Passage – for in fact there are several – sailed under Sir John Franklin, a captain in the Royal Navy. In 1845, Sir John left the Port of London, in command of *Erebus* and *Terror*, two converted naval "bomb ships". About three years later some of his men reached Simpson Strait, discovered previously by Dr George Simpson, of the Hudson's Bay Company, working from the west. Unfortunately Franklin's story had to be unearthed by subsequent search expeditions. His ships were lost in the villainous pack ice of Victoria Strait. He and his followers perished, every one.

Nonetheless, it was Franklin's example, so Amundsen afterwards maintained, that at the age of fifteen, originally inspired him to become a polar explorer.

> Oddly enough [he wrote], it was the sufferings that Sir John and his men had to go through which attracted me most in his narrative. A strange urge made me wish that I too one day would go through the same thing. Perhaps it was the idealism of youth, which often takes the form of martyrdom, that got me to see myself as a kind of crusader in Arctic exploration. I also wanted to suffer for a cause – not in a burning desert on the way to Jerusalem – but in the frosty North.

Any lingering relics of such morbid adolescent longings were effectively cured by Amundsen's harrowing experiences on *Belgica*. Nonetheless his ambition to do the North West Passage persisted. Although Franklin and his successors had charted the various alternatives, it was as sledge travellers over frozen waterways. Nobody had yet taken one and the same ship through from end to end. *That* would be the true culmination of the historic quest and that, Amundsen decided, was what he was going to do.

On *Belgica*, when, as Amundsen dispassionately noted, there was "just as great a chance of remaining beset in the ice as ever getting out",

> our original plan of determining the position of the South Magnetic Pole was constantly discussed, and that led in turn to the . . . position of the North Magnetic Pole also being passionately debated. Some of the scientists on board considered that the position of the North Magnetic Pole had been established once and for all by Sir James Clark Ross in 1831, while others believed that it had moved in the course of time. These discussions awoke my burning interest [and] I was overcome more and more by a desire to go to the North American Arctic, and investigate the conditions round the North Magnetic Pole, where no one had been since Ross.

Such at least was the way that Amundsen spoke to the Norwegian Geographical Society in 1901. It was two years since his return from the *Belgica* and the end of a stage in his polar apprenticeship. Now, for the first time, both as ship's captain and leader, he was proceeding to organize an expedition of his own.

In October 1902, Sir Clements Markham, President of the Royal Geographical Society in London, and a power in geographical circles, was visiting Christiania. One afternoon, he met Nansen and Amundsen and, in his own words,

> we all three went down to where the little vessel . . . was lying, in which Amundsen is going to the North Magnetic Pole. He has called her the *Gjøa* [47 tons] 70 feet long by 20. He has put a little engine into her, worked with petroleum, which will make her go 5 knots . . . we went for a short cruise in the fjord . . . Nansen has a high opinion of young Amundsen.

The North Magnetic Pole happened to lie somewhere along the North West Passage. As a façade of respectability it would do; Amundsen had grasped that to obtain a serious hearing, exploration now had to be dressed up in scientific clothes. In any case, for fear of courting failure, he shrank from revealing his true intentions. To the world, he was sailing in search of the North Magnetic Pole. The North West Passage remained his own, very private aspiration.

Money was Amundsen's problem, for a businessman he was not. He proposed paying what he could and, for the rest, as he once told Nansen, "I will have to depend on my credit and good fortune." He had spent nearly his whole inheritance on *Gjøa*. Intermediaries secured a little help from wealthy sympathizers. Nonetheless, in the summer of 1903, as sailing day approached, Amundsen found himself enmeshed in debt. Creditors demanded instant payment. Some threatened writs to prevent *Gjøa* sailing. Amundsen was worn out with their distasteful attentions.

Well-wishers helped with a last-minute loan. Nansen paid a few pressing bills, and talked the most importunate creditors into holding their hand. Late in the evening of the 16th June, so the story goes, he arrived post haste in a horse and carriage at *Gjøa*'s moorings, advised Amundsen to get away while the going was good, and galloped off home again.

A few hours later, at midnight, Amundsen cast off. Unobserved, through pouring rain, *Gjøa* slipped away from Christiania down the fjord towards the open sea. When the Norwegian coast finally sank astern, Amundsen appeared with a bottle of rum, and poured out drinks all round. "Well, boys, we're clear of the creditors," one of the crew recalled his saying. "Skål and bon voyage."

Franklin and his successors had been martyrs to rigid minds and bungling. Amundsen was determined to learn from their mistakes. "What has not been accomplished with large vessels and main force," as he put it, "I will attempt with a small vessel and patience." *Gjøa* was one eighth the size of just one of Franklin's ships. Where Franklin had 128 men, Amundsen was taking exactly six.

*Gjøa* headed first for Godhavn, in Northern Greenland, there to take on board "10 really good dogs, well trained in hauling sledges", as Amundsen had previously ordered from the authorities in Copenhagen.

> Since my journey will probably take 4 years, it would be helpful to have dogs of both sexes, so that reproduction can take place en route.

Amundsen recoiled from the martyrdom of man-hauling, to which, in a spirit of self-mortification, official British explorers had been addicted.

From Godhavn, Amundsen continued north along the Greenland coast to load 105 packing cases with supplies dumped for him in advance by Scots whalers on an offshore islet called Dalrymple Rock. Deep laden now, with frighteningly low freeboard, *Gjøa* headed across Baffin Bay for the Canadian side, and Lancaster Sound, the start of the North West Passage proper.

On the 22nd August, *Gjøa* dropped anchor in Erebus Bay on Beechey Island, the first of Franklin's wintering stations. So far the voyage, as Amundsen put it, "resembled a holiday excursion". Notoriously stormy waters had stayed calm. Pack ice obediently opened up for him. This state of affairs persisted as *Gjøa* sailed along Peel Sound, through Franklin Strait, and passed the furthest point yet reached by any ship before. Where tight packed ice had barred his predecessors, Amundsen found open waters. "Are we really going to get through so easily?" he incredulously asked in his diary.

An answer of a kind soon emerged. On the 31st August, *Gjøa* ran aground off the Beaufort Islands, in the James Ross Strait, but soon floated free. Next day, there was a fire in the engine room, extinguished without much damage. This was followed by a violent northerly gale and, early in the morning of the 3rd September, *Gjøa* ran aground again.

She was jammed on an uncharted reef off Matty Isle, and this time seemed stuck for good. "As always in difficult situations," wrote Amundsen, "I conferred with my companions," and they tried in vain to sail *Gjøa* off. After two days, Amundsen prepared to abandon ship but, urged on by Anton Lund, the first mate, as a last resort he tried jettisoning the deck cargo. The wind then obligingly veered to the right quarter and, in her lightened state, *Gjøa* was blown off to float again. Had the wind shifted, or *Gjøa* drawn two feet more, nobody would have lived to tell the tale.

Further on, Amundsen found Simpson Strait enticingly free of ice. The North West Passage, as he put it,

> was thus open for us. But our aim was first and foremost the North Magnetic Pole – so the Passage would just have to wait.

Amundsen put *Gjøa* into a natural harbour on King William Land – Gjøahaven, he called it – and let her freeze in for the winter.

Early in April 1904, with Peder Ristvedt, *Gjøa*'s chief engineer, Amundsen set out for the North Magnetic Pole. As far as he could tell from his instruments, he was in the vicinity of that fugitive point during May. It was now well north along the Boothia Peninsular, and had undoubtedly moved since Ross was there, some seventy years before.

On the 28th May, when Amundsen returned to *Gjøa*, he had covered less than 500 miles, including false starts, but he had learned much about travel over snow and ice, especially dog driving. Despite his protestations, that meant far more to him than the Magnetic Pole.

Amundsen's real concern was with the surrounding Eskimos. Since autumn 1903, he had carefully cultivated their acquaintance. These Eskimos were Netsiliks, and had hardly seen *Kabluna*, as they called white men, before. Amundsen carefully observed them. Untrained as he was, his notes and his collection of artefacts show a natural aptitude for ethnography. His interest was far from academic. He wanted to learn the art of survival in a polar climate. He was unusual among polar explorers in grasping that the Eskimos were not savages, but highly adapted to their surroundings, with much to teach. Nor did he romanticize them. At one point he blew up an old igloo with dynamite to impress them with the white man's power.

Amundsen, as he said, felt "much melancholy" when, on the 13th August 1905, he sailed out of Gjøahaven, after a stay of almost two years. For their part, the Eskimos came down to say farewell.

> I am not sure that the little brown-eyed people on the beach were quite cheerful that morning [Amundsen wrote]. They waved long to us – probably a farewell for life; and if some traveller, many years later, pays this place a visit, the numerous tent-rings will remind him of the many happy days the *Gjøa* expedition spent here with their friends the Netsilik Eskimos.

Ahead now lay Simpson Strait, an uncharted labyrinth of shoals, drifting ice and treacherous currents, through which no ship had yet sailed. With the lead going all the time, and the crew standing watch and watch, *Gjøa* crawled safely through. After four days, she passed Cape Colborne, the furthest point yet reached by any ship coming from the west. Amundsen had linked the work of centuries and completed the North West Passage.

Still there were miles of foul and sketchily charted channels with which to contend. On the morning of the 26th August, *Gjøa* at last found comparatively safe waters in what was later called Amundsen Gulf. It ought to have been a moment of elation; but since leaving Gjøahaven a fortnight before, Amundsen had been under an intolerable strain. At any time, *Gjøa* might have foundered on an unsuspected shoal. Now, he was overcome by a reaction and went down below to sleep.

"At 11 a.m. I was woken by a shout of 'ship ahead'," his diary records.

> I was not slow to go topsides. It was a schooner, "Charles Hansson" of San Francisco, Captain James McKenna . . . How surprised was I not, when Captain McKenna wrapped his fist round mine and congratulated me on a brilliant success.

At King Point, on the Yukon Coast of Canada, *Gjøa* was stopped by ice, and frozen in for a third winter. This was not at all to Amundsen's taste. He hoped to clear his debts with newspaper contracts, and had to get his news through as quickly as he could. At Herschel Island, not far off, some American whalers were wintering. On 24th October two Eskimos left for the interior with post. With them was William Mogg, a shipwrecked whaling captain, who was financing the journey. They were joined by Amundsen.

On the 5th December, Amundsen reached Eagle City, far down the Yukon, in Alaska. Five hundred miles from King Point, it was the nearest telegraph station on Amundsen's route. There, he sent his telegram announcing the conquest of the North West Passage, and awoke, although he did not know it, a famous man. Unfortunately the telegram was leaked along the way, American newspapers pirated the story, and it was widely reprinted. Consequently, the legitimate recipients, including *The Times* of London, who had contracted for exclusive rights, declined to pay. For Amundsen, it was a depressing financial blow, but he swallowed his disappointment and, after waiting two months in Eagle City for post, started the return journey to *Gjøa* on the 3rd February 1906. He arrived on the 12th March, having skied the whole 1,000 miles to Eagle City and back. This involved two crossings of the windswept Brooks mountain range, near the coast, and a long haul through forests buried in loose snow, besides going up and down the Porcupine and Yukon rivers, in difficult conditions. It was a considerable journey in its own right, and another stage in Amundsen's polar preparation. Along the way, as he put it, he had "every opportunity to become acquainted with the generous hospitality of Alaska".

Little was left now, except to wait for the ice to thaw. Occasionally, Amundsen visited the whaling captains at Herschel Island. "They all bore the stamp of the life they lead in these regions," he observed, "and were corpulent, with thinning hair." They had motley crews and, as Amundsen commented darkly, "there can scarcely be any doubt that conditions on these American whalers are not what they ought to be."

Amundsen was relieved when, finally, on the 10th July, *Gjøa* left King Point, to make her way through the ice, and between the shoals of the north coast of Alaska. On 30th August, she passed through the Bering Strait, and left the Arctic, running before a storm. As Amundsen had begun the enterprise, so he ended it with a skål:

> I had thought of celebrating our passage through the Bering Strait [Amundsen wrote in his diary], but we could just manage a little glass of whisky on deck in a hurry – there was no question of flying a flag. It was with happiness we emptied our glasses, for whatever happens now, we have brought the Norwegian flag through the North-West Passage on *one* ship.

In the end, Amundsen's painstaking magnetic observations proved all but useless. It was as the first man to sail through the North West Passage that he achieved fame. His enduring monument was the collection of Netsilik artefacts he brought back. He had proved his real metier to be ethnography.

In the words of Major General Adolphus Greely, an American contemporary of Amundsen's, and a well known Arctic explorer, the North West Passage

> has ruined reputations, bestowed honours . . . and cost scores of lives . . . the voyage of Amundsen stands forth unrivalled as to scant means . . . and successful navigation . . . these results have been produced by the labour of only [seven] men, without undue suffering . . . The outcome stamps Amundsen as a man endowed with high qualities of administration, judgment, and resourcefulness.

On the 15th August 1903, while approaching Dalrymple Rock, off the coast of Greenland, Amundsen noted in his diary that he

> heard a loud volley of rifle fire, and 6 slender kayaks appeared from behind an iceberg. 2 of them bore little flags at their bows, the one the Danish, and the other the Norwegian. It was Mylius-Erichsen . . . and . . . Knud Rasmussen, together with 4 Eskimos.

Mylius-Erichsen was the leader of the Danish so-called "literary" expedition collecting the folk tales of the Eskimo. He was marooned for the winter, but nonetheless pressed on Amundsen four of his best sledge dogs. Amundsen requited by sharing some of his delicacies. That included a bottle of his own slender stock of rather good red wine, which Mylius-Erichsen, to his everlasting chagrin, accidentally broke, spilling the contents on the beach.

Mylius-Erichsen remembered Amundsen as "an extraordinarily powerful man. Rarely have I seen hands so hardened by work as his." Count Harald Moltke, one of his companions, vividly recalled "Captain Amundsen with the aquiline nose".

Godfred Hansen, Amundsen's second-in-command, and a lone Dane among the Norwegians, had met Moltke before. "How odd that we had to meet at the edge of the world," Hansen remarked, "after living for 10 years next door without seeing each other." Hansen was a dedicated amateur photographer, and recorded the chance encounter. This picture shows members of the Danish expedition on board *Gjøa*. Mylius-Erichsen is standing on the extreme right. Next to him is Jørgen Brønlund, followed by Knud Rasmussen.

The memorial on Beechey Island, where Sir John Franklin wintered in 1845–6. This was one of the slides Amundsen showed in his lecture to the Royal Geographical Society in London in February 1907. Beechey Island, he told his audience,

> gives a barren and dismal impression; and particularly sad are the ruins of the house erected by the British Government for the succour of the Franklin Expedition. Five graves did not make it any more cheerful. The memorial stone to Sir John Franklin was the only thing which in the least brightened all this sadness – a handsome marble tablet, put up to his memory by his faithful wife.

For Amundsen, Beechey Island was the crossroads: which way should he now proceed? "It seems that the Magnetic Pole has more or less kept its old position," he wrote in his diary, after consulting his instruments, "and on that account I have decided to sail along Peel Sound."

Unloading *Gjøa* at Gjøahaven.

"The human factor," Amundsen liked to say, "is three quarters of any expedition." He chose his men carefully.

On the North West Passage, Gustav Juel Wiik (*left*), was nonetheless reprimanded in the expedition journal for "privately bartering expedition equipment [with] the Eskimos", thereupon asking Amundsen "if he had any complaints over his, Wiik's moral behaviour."

Amundsen had been disillusioned to find the Eskimos "dealing in women", as he put it. "I was offered masses of women very cheaply." Wiik was suspected of accepting similar propositions. Amundsen disapproved, partly because a visiting Eskimo had been found to be suffering from syphilis.

> I called my men together [Amundsen noted laconically], and told them all this, adding that I assumed the disease to be widespread in the tribe.

Godfred Hansen (*right*), the second-in-command, was a Danish naval lieutenant from Copenhagen. "I was not taken for my qualifications," he ironically remarked, "but because no Norwegian naval officer had volunteered." Amundsen wanted a naval officer, because of superior theoretical training, and dependability in taking observations.

Amundsen told the RGS that Godfred Hansen's

> light-hearted disposition was of absolute benefit to us, and during the . . . more than three years that he and I spent together in the little cabin of the *Gjøa*, 6 × 9 feet, I became more and more attached to him. It was prophesied before our departure from Norway, that within a year we should not be able to bear the sight of one another; this prophecy, however, we thoroughly gave the lie to.

When *Gjøa* ran aground during a storm in James Ross Strait, Anton Lund (*left*), the first mate, virtually seized command, and saved her from shipwreck. Amundsen afterwards thanked Lund for his initiative.

Besides being the oldest on board Lund was also incontestably the most experienced and able seaman. Born in 1864, he came from Tromsø, in northern Norway. He was a sealing skipper, and had sailed the Arctic for twenty-five years.

Amundsen also admired Lund for the way he helped to devise employment during the long, dark winters. "On a polar expedition . . . idleness can be quite demoralizing. For that reason alone, it is inadvisable to have too many people . . . to find work for a huge crowd would be virtually impossible."

Helmer Hanssen (*right*), *Gjøa*'s second mate, came from the Vesterålen Islands in northern Norway. He too had sailed the Arctic as a sealer. On the North West Passage, learning from the Eskimos, he made himself a master of dog driving. He became the best dog driver on the expedition.

Hanssen first met Amundsen in 1897, when Amundsen was about to sail to the Antarctic in *Belgica*. "Little did I know," said Hanssen, "that I was to be connected with him and his expeditions for all of eighteen years." Five years later he heard that a berth was vacant on *Gjøa*, applied, and was immediately accepted. He went to the polar regions, so he said, because, since childhood, he had wanted to "get out and see the world".

Amundsen (left), Helmer Hanssen and Peder Ristvedt, in the saloon of *Gjøa*, February 1904. They are wearing Netsilik reindeer fur anoraks. Amundsen had acquired complete Netsilik outfits, and "begun to go around dressed completely as an Eskimo", he wrote in his diary.

> Both inner and outer anoraks hang loosely outside the trousers . . . so that the air can circulate freely. I find it excellent, and the only way to wear fur clothes, if one is to avoid sweating. Now I can move as I want to. Am always warm, without sweating.

Amundsen had persuaded Teraiu, a Netsilik, to teach him igloo building; for a fee of one empty tin per lesson. Teraiu laughed at his efforts, but soon after starting the course, Amundsen noted: "Temperature −30°C. Feels like summer. During the morning built igloo with Helmer Hanssen – four man model – in 1hr.15mins."

Amundsen was absorbing Eskimo techniques in preparation for his forthcoming journey to the North Magnetic Pole. Amongst other things, he learned how to coat sledge runners with a thin, flexible layer of ice, in order to overcome the sand-like friction of very cold drift snow. "Going native" was unusual among polar explorers, but Amundsen owed much to an earlier example. In the second quarter of the nineteenth century, Dr John Rae, an Orkneyman working in the Canadian Arctic, pioneered the small expedition, living like the Eskimos. He set an example of achieving much with small means, but he was best known abroad. At home, of course, he was completely neglected.

Amundsen, in his own words, set Ristvedt to "making lightweight trade goods; knives, arrowheads, etc., to take along on our sledge journeys". This was to trade for more artefacts with Eskimos they might meet along the way. Amundsen had deliberately arranged for the work to be done on the expedition, instead of bringing ready made goods. This was to help keep his men occupied. Besides, he wanted to see what would really be useful to the Eskimos. He did not want to pervert their taste with gaudy trinkets.

Ristvedt needed no convincing. "The Eskimos were wonderful people," as he put it.

> When Amundsen talked about the Eskimos, he often finished by saying: "The best wish I have for my friends the Eskimos is that civilization never reaches them." I say the same.

Ristvedt had originally been Amundsen's sergeant during his military service. Amundsen was so impressed with his versatility that he asked Ristvedt to join the expedition. Ristvedt mustered as chief engineer. Before sailing, he made the pemmican, for Amundsen did not trust commercial products.

Netsilik Eskimo visitors to *Gjøa*. The figure on the extreme right is Umiktuallu, nicknamed "The murderer", because he killed a foster-son in a vendetta.

Amundsen's diary for 29th October 1903 reads:

Up on the hillside to the north I saw a herd of what I first assumed to be reindeer, but which on more careful examination turned out to be human beings. Our first Eskimos. I got ready with all possible speed and ordered Lund and Hanssen to follow me with rifles . . . The Eskimos . . . advanced directly to us in a line. Without a trace of fear they came closer, and about 100 metres from the vessel we met . . . They gave their greetings of friendship by rubbing us on the chest and shouting in chorus: *"Minaktumi."* We did the same, and our friendship was sealed.

Soon Amundsen was writing that

We are steadily bartering for Eskimo clothes. These garments are extraordinarily beautiful. The ethnographic collection increases steadily . . . The plague, generally mentioned in connection with Eskimos, namely, lice, is not found among these.

None of these Eskimos had seen a white man before. Amundsen showed them copies of the *Illustrated London News*:

They are all from the Boer War, and mostly show battle scenes. It is amusing to see how the Eskimos associate all these pictures with reindeer hunting.

Gustav Wiik, in full Netsilik reindeer outfit. Reindeer fur is one of the best natural insulating materials, and the Eskimos anticipated modern cold weather clothing by using successive layers to build up insulation. Amundsen observed that European clothes could not be combined with Eskimo fur garments. Wool undergarments made one "sweaty"; it had to be fur all the way. He also found that in very cold weather, bearskin mittens were superior to reindeer fur. He was constantly experimenting; trying to learn for the future.

Wiik was responsible for magnetic observations on *Gjøa*. In his lecture to the RGS, Amundsen explained that Wiik went through a course of instruction at the magnetic observatory at Potsdam, and praised his "painstaking and accurate labour". During the expedition, however, Amundsen observed in his diary that Wiik complained that his hands could not stand work in the cold . . . Aptitude and training are useful, but accuracy and understanding of how to use an instrument are possibly better.

Moreover, in the expedition log, Wiik was reprimanded for unsatisfactory work. He had to take some of the blame for poor scientific results.

Wiik tragically died on the 31st March 1906, during the third year of the expedition. There was no doctor with Amundsen, so that proper treatment was unavailable, and any diagnosis uncertain. From Amundsen's description, it might have been appendicitis; but he feared something contagious.

*Left*] Departure, 1st March 1904, on the first attempt to reach the North Magnetic Pole. It ended after four days, and less than 10 miles. Amundsen baldly summed up:

> On this tour, short as it was, we nonetheless gained experience. [It] was due . . . to our splendid little igloo . . . that we were able to spend a pleasant night out at −61.5°C.

At such low temperatures, the sledges would not slide. Because there were too few dogs and too many men, one sledge had to be man-hauled. One day, in Amundsen's own words,

> by offering all our strength, we managed to advance 3½ miles. This was disheartening. Both animals and men are hard put to cope with such conditions. The cold is bad enough, but virtually not being able to move is worse.

From that moment, Amundsen feared man-hauling, and learned to depend on dogs.

*Above*] The magnetic dip needle in a "half igloo" during the third, and more or less successful attempt to reach the North Magnetic Pole, April–May 1904. When the needle approaches the vertical, the Magnetic Pole must be in the vicinity.

Amundsen had spent several months, both at the German Hydrographic Office in Hamburg and the magnetic observatory at Potsdam. In the event, as he himself admitted, "I do not have enough knowledge of terrestrial magnetism." The results were largely valueless. To Amundsen, science on an expedition henceforth seemed a snare and a delusion. He preferred pure geographical discovery.

Two pictures of Amundsen's tent at the North Magnetic Pole, Boothia Peninsula, May 1904. His companion on this journey was Ristvedt, much appreciated for his sense of humour. At one point, the dogs, Amundsen wrote in his diary, were

> turning up their noses at pemmican. They consider old pieces of fur a delicacy. "The menu of the Polar dog is comprehensive," said Ristvedt. "I think I can manage many dishes, but I don't think I could have managed your old underpants." The dogs smacked their lips over them like a bear with honey.

Ristvedt's real worth to the expedition was his gift for putting people at their ease. Like Amundsen, he was happiest with small groups. By common consent, his personality matched that of Amundsen's, and he was in a way the real second in command. Of him, Godfred Hansen said that he owed much to his "mental balance, even humour, good marksmanship and unshakeable courage".

It was Ristvedt who largely fed his companions with the reindeer that he shot.

During the journey to the Magnetic Pole, Ristvedt returned with dogs and sledge to Gjøa to replace a broken chronometer, leaving Amundsen to guard their camp from plundering by Eskimos. "Ristvedt left on Saturday at 10 p.m.," Amundsen recorded on the 20th April.

> He reached Ogluli [The Eskimo name for Gjøahaven] at 10 a.m. on Sunday, a distance of 54 nautical miles . . . He returned this evening [Wednesday] . . . I am really glad to have Ristvedt here again. It was too long in inactivity.

The Magnetic Poles of the Earth are not points, as Amundsen well knew. They are nebulous and shifting areas. Ristvedt graphically described the search:

> We moved and observed; moved and observed and [the pole] moved. In the evening . . . we could be quite near the pole, we believed. But next morning the needle swung far off.

Within certain limits, therefore, the date of arrival was elastic. Amundsen chose 17th May, the Norwegian national day. His diary reads:

> The festive day opened with SE breeze. First, of course, we opened the mysterious box [sent by Lindstrøm, the cook]. Its contents were: 1 fish pudding, 1 caramel pudding, 1 ptarmigan paté, cakes and cigars . . . a banquet [and] besides . . . the remaining maraschino. We could thus drink all the usual skåls – the King, Fatherland etc . . . The tent was dressed with flags . . . The dogs also felt the significance of the day; each had his ptarmigan wing. This went down like hot cakes.

Netsilik Eskimo about to go salmon fishing, King William Land, summer 1905. Amundsen described the process in his diary:

> Salmon is found just about everywhere. [The Eskimo uses] a *Navlingiun*. This consists of two parts: the shaft, a narrow, round wooden stick about 2 m. long, sharpened at one end. This fits into a socket at one end of a spearhead, made of reindeer antler, about 30 cm. long, and round cross-section, which can be considered an extension of the shaft. It narrows evenly, and ends in a sharp point. On each side, there is a row of backward facing flukes. The socket in which the shaft rests, is quite shallow, so that the two parts can easily separate from each other. The outer part is secured to the shaft with a thin, braided line of reindeer sinew. In the middle of the shaft, another line is attached, this also made of reindeer sinews. When the salmon is speared, his lively movements make certain that the two parts [of the weapon] separate quickly, and all strain is taken by the line. [The weapon] is not thrown, but thrust into the fish. Usually [the Eskimo] approaches the fish very closely.

The purpose of this remarkably sophisticated device is to avoid breaking the shaft, for wood was precious in these surroundings. At that time, the only regular source was driftwood. It is a good example of the technical basis of the Netsilik culture – and of Amundsen's power of observation.

Between the 2nd April and 25th June 1905, Godfred Hansen and Peder Ristvedt explored the coast of Victoria Land, one of the last uncharted stretches of the North American continent. The picture shows Ristvedt with his dog team, probably near Cape Nansen, their furthest point.

"I thought that our journey was of great significance," Hansen said afterwards.

Because even if the coast along which we travelled was a coast of iron; stormy, fog-covered, icebound summer and winter; nonetheless it was the land we had wrested from the grip of darkness and drawn in our chart. Arid and stony as it was, without any beauty of its own, without any use for human kind, nonetheless it seemed to me that out of the interminable wilderness were born great and beautiful and good thoughts, and that is what I wanted to write about. I wanted to write, so that those who read would, as it were, have gained some impression of immensity, such as I have acquired in those places, where there are no roads, but where God's sun, or the glittering stars show the way ahead. Now that the work is done, I see how little I have managed to convey, because those thoughts which seemed to pour over me at the time, were not thoughts to be expressed in words, but mostly moods.

Jimmi (*opposite*) a Kagmallik Eskimo and Kappa (*above*), his wife, with whom Amundsen travelled to Eagle City, Alaska, to send his cable on the attainment of the North West Passage. They started on the 24th October 1905 from Herschel Island.

Jimmi, Amundsen wrote along the way, was

an excellent man. Friendly and polite – helpful at all times, and Kappa . . . not less so. She was a "kabluna woman" [White man's concubine] . . . before marrying her present husband, so she is fairly civilized. She manages English fairly well. Relations between man and wife are excellent.

This journey taught Amundsen more about snow travel.

Once across the coastal mountains, he found

the most troublesome terrain one can imagine. The snow always lies very loosely in these parts. Ski are continually caught in the vegetation.

On the 5th December Amundsen, with Captain Mogg, the shipwrecked whaling captain from Herschel Island, reached Eagle City. Amundsen wrote that they were

received in a very friendly manner by Major Plumer, the commanding [U.S. Army] officer. He accompanied us to the telegraph station . . . and we sent our telegrams . . . we went home with the second in command [where] we had a good wash, had our hair cut, and were shaved by his barber, and were put into some of his clothes.

Eskimo graves on Herschel Island. Amundsen wrote that they

made a strange impression. It was almost as if some merchant had exhibited his wares at this place. Eskimos lay their dead in an ordinary wooden box, which they put in the graveyard in rows on the ground.

When he lectured to the Royal Geographical Society, Amundsen explained that

the religious opinions of the Eskimo were like our own in that they had an understanding of a good and evil being, of punishment and reward. If a man behaved as he should in this life, then he would go to the hunting fields in the moon; and had he been a bad man he must go under the earth . . . suicide . . . is not considered to be wrong.

Villa Magneten, Amundsen's magnetic observatory at Gjøahaven, 1903–5. It was built of special non-magnetic packing cases, originally used for supplies. No iron was used in their construction, and all nails were of bronze.

Villa Magneten gave Amundsen his first contact with his future rival, Captain Scott. Simultaneous magnetic observations had been arranged between Amundsen and Scott, then at the other end of the world, commanding the *Discovery* in the Antarctic. The agreed periods were known as "term days". On the 1st November 1903, Amundsen noted in his diary:

> Today we should have participated in the international "term day" in connection with "Discovery" – the English south polar expedition – but due to a regrettable mistake, we missed it. In our rush, we mistook 12 noon for 12 midnight. We thus will not have the opportunity of taking part in more than the 3 last term days.

Manni, an Eskimo boy, on board *Gjøa*. Amundsen wanted to bring him back to Norway and have him educated. Godfred Hansen had started to teach him to read and write, but Manni was not sure whether he really wanted to go. He was drowned in an accident off Herschel Island in 1906, just as *Gjøa* was about to sail for Bering Strait, and San Francisco, where her voyage ended.

# II

# *THE SOUTH POLE EXPEDITION*

## 1910–1912

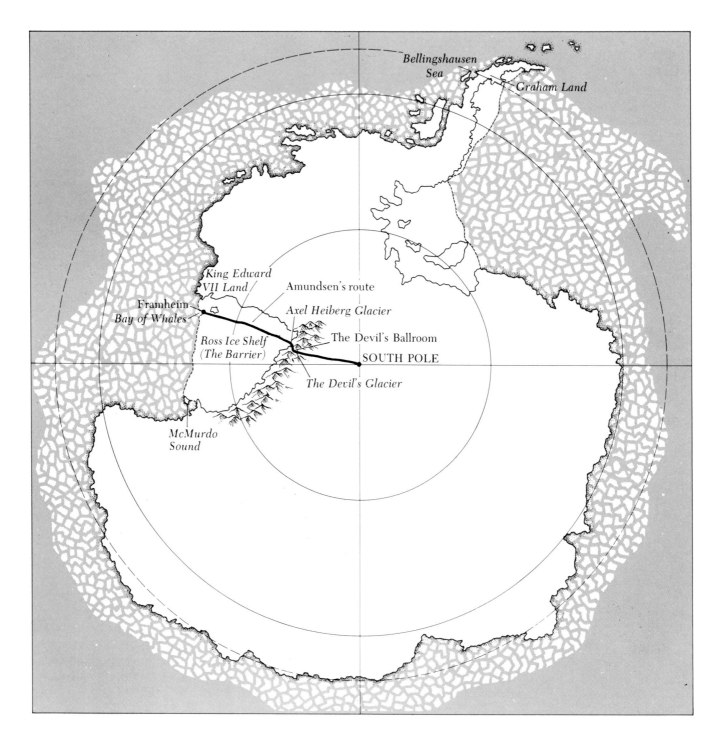

# THE SOUTH POLE
# EXPEDITION

In the autumn of 1907, with his boxes of lantern slides, Amundsen toured America to lecture on the North West Passage. He opened in New York which, as he succinctly wrote, was "a cold douche . . . 2 to 300 people were all that were present in Carnegie Hall, which can hold as many thousands." Things were better in Philadelphia where, said Amundsen,

> The house was full . . . a most refined and understanding audience. It is a pleasure to give a lecture under such circumstances.

He was soon reporting "Full houses everywhere." More to the point, the takings were not being swallowed up by old debts.

Amundsen had returned home to Norway in November 1906, having attained the North West Passage, and achieved his ambition, but with satisfaction still mysteriously elusive. He looked for new worlds to conquer.

However he was fêted, to Amundsen himself, the North West Passage simply meant another stage in his professional training. After twenty years of preparation, he felt reasonably qualified at last, and now he wanted the yet unattained North Pole itself.

The American, Robert Peary, had just returned from his second attempt to reach the Pole. Amundsen, however, was not exactly following in his footsteps. Peary used a route starting from Cape Columbia, at the tip of the North American continent. Amundsen modelled himself instead on Fridtjof Nansen.

A decade earlier, Nansen had taken a specially built ship called *Fram* ("Forwards"), deliberately allowed her to be frozen in, and drifted across the Arctic in the polar pack ice. At a certain point, together with a single companion, he had left the ship and, using ski and dogs, made a dash for the North Pole. The advantage of this method was that the ship itself gained latitude, shortening the distance to be covered by men and dogs. The drawback was the difficulty of return.

Nansen reached 86°14′N, a record at the time. Amundsen proposed to repeat Nansen's expedition, but on another line of drift, so that the ship would reach a higher latitude, and the North Pole consequently be closer for the final dash. In November 1908, he announced his new expedition.

Amundsen wanted *Fram*. She had been taken over by the state, but Nansen still had first call on her use, and he was hankering after the South Pole. Nonetheless, after some hesitation, he ceded his claim in favour of Amundsen.

Amundsen had returned from the North West Passage, as he had set out, in debt. There was this difference, however; he had left in obscurity, and come back in fame. Moreover, in 1905, while he was still away, Norway had finally secured independence from Sweden, and Amundsen became a symbol of national identity and national prestige. In 1907, the Norwegian Government gave him 40,000 kroner to clear outstanding liabilities.

Still, Amundsen had to find the money for his new enterprise. His lectures in America on the North West Passage helped. So too did the royalties on *The North West Passage*, the book of the expedition; but not enough. By the beginning of 1909, he had scarcely collected a quarter of the money he needed and, in a year, he was supposed to sail. On this occasion, his family could not help. Repugnant as he found it, Amundsen was forced to ask the Norwegian Government for further help. He was rewarded with a grant of 75,000 kroner to give *Fram* a very necessary refit.

Despite royal patronage, and a few rich backers, money was still lacking. The resemblance to the start of the North West Passage was too close for comfort. Once more, Amundsen raised credit by the use of Nansen's name – besides his own – and cheerfully continued with his preparations.

The lessons learned on the North West Passage were meticulously applied. Every item of equipment was specially designed. Anoraks were sewn on the pattern of the Netsilik Eskimos'. Food was carefully prepared. With equal thoroughness, Amundsen chose his men. Helmer Hanssen and Adolf Lindstrøm, from the North West Passage, were coming again. In all respects, except finance, Amundsen was doing well.

Then, in the first week of September, Peary and Dr F. A. Cook appeared from out of the Arctic, each claiming to have reached the North Pole. Amundsen hurriedly left Christiania for Copenhagen, ostensibly to meet Dr Cook, his old shipmate from *Belgica*.

Cook was in Copenhagen, because he had returned to

civilization in a Danish ship from Greenland. In his own words, he advised Amundsen

> against the execution of [his] enterprise . . . I said that the North Pole is now out of the picture. Why not try for the South Pole. This for a moment almost took Amundsen's breath. He sat in meditation for a while . . . Then [he] said . . . this is the thing to do. Let me think it over.

Amundsen, on the other hand, later told a companion that it was

> not really to meet Cook that he went down to Copenhagen . . . but to secure 100 huskies from Greenland through the [Danish] Government, to be used in an attempt on the South Pole.

By the time Amundsen left Copenhagen on Saturday 11th September, and sailed through the Narrows, under Hamlet's castle at Elsinore, he *had* ordered one hundred dogs from Greenland, he had undoubtedly decided to turn south, and he had not announced his change of plan. On Monday, in Christiania, he was confronted with unexpected, and not wholly agreeable news. Captain Robert Falcon Scott was to lead an English attempt on the South Pole.

Amundsen had been fleetingly concerned with Scott during the magnetic term days on the North West Passage, but they had never met. By reputation, however, Amundsen knew Scott to be a jealous man. Scott had tried to stop Sir Ernest Shackleton, his celebrated rival, making an attempt on the South Pole from what he regarded as his, Scott's territory in the Ross Sea. Amundsen felt at an even greater disadvantage, for Scott was an officer of the then mightiest navy in the world, and Britain was one of the great powers, while Norway was but a small and newly independent country.

Amundsen also feared that his Norwegian backers might object to his change of plan, withdrawing their support, or even stopping him altogether. Threatened on all sides, he was driven to concealment. He pretended he was still going north; in secret, he now prepared to go south.

When Cook and Peary returned, the heart had gone out of Amundsen's original enterprise. His talk of a scientific expedition to the Arctic basin was a hollow pretence. As he once frankly said, he could never understand "why anyone should want to go to a place where somebody else had been . . . or go there for the sake of doing it a different way".

Peary was soon accusing Cook of having perpetrated a hoax, and officially was adjudged the sole conqueror of the North Pole, but there remained doubts about the claims of both, unsettled to this day. The one certainty was that no one else could ever claim uncontested primacy again. That could not be said of the South Pole. In January 1909, Shackleton had got within ninety-seven miles, or thereabouts. More than anyone else, Shackleton had

"managed to lift the veil resting over Antarctica", as Amundsen put it. "But a little corner still remained."

For a whole year, Amundsen had to keep his secret. He was compelled to share it with his brother Leon, who acted as his business manager, and also with Lt. Thorvald Nilsen, a Norwegian naval officer who was *Fram*'s captain, and had to prepare his navigation in advance. On the eve of departure, a few others were also told. Nonetheless when, like a Viking ship slipping out on a raid, *Fram* sailed from Kristiansand, and left Norway on the 9th August 1910, not a whisper of her true destination had leaked out. Even her crew thought they were still heading north.

It was, Amundsen wrote, "a wonderful feeling to cast off at last, and head for my goal". He had gone through appalling strain. He had had to dissemble, to watch every step, weigh every word and yet, because of his nature, to avoid the lie direct. By comparison, the fact that he had departed once more in debt was a minor inconvenience.

On the 6th September, a Tuesday, *Fram* reached Madeira, and anchored in Funchal Roads. Amundsen's brother Leon, having gone on ahead, was there to meet him. On Friday evening, in Amundsen's own words:

> At 6 o'clock I called all hands on deck and announced my intention of heading for the South Pole. When I asked if they were willing to follow me, I received a unanimous "yes".

This bald note in Amundsen's diary hid considerable drama. Madeira was the parting of the ways. When *Fram* sailed, she would not touch land again until she reached Antarctica.

> Leon was then the only non-participant on board [Amundsen continued in his diary]. After the announcement, each man had time to write home with the news. At 9 o'clock L. left us. He had with him all the post. That will be delivered when the plan is published . . . At 9.30 we raised anchor and stood out to sea under power. It was clear, with a starlit sky – a wonderful night. Half an hour later, we were in the N.E. Trade Wind – fresh and free. We hoisted sail, and are now making a good speed for – the South Pole.

Amundsen reminded his men that they were now racing the English. "That means we'll get there first!" one of them had replied. The speaker happened to be Olav Bjaaland, a Norwegian ski champion, and one of the finest Nordic skiers of the age. Reaching the South Pole would simply be the longest cross-country ski race in history, and Norwegians were obviously better skiers than anyone else. Nonetheless, as Amundsen always said:

> Only the most careful planning . . . and endless patience in working out the tiniest details of equipment, will ensure a fortunate outcome.

Although *Fram* rolled like a demented turtle, Amundsen was grateful for every moment on board, because it meant much needed time to complete vital preparations. For his original Arctic drift, he had deliberately left a great deal of work for the long winters in the ice. Now, most of it had to be crammed into the voyage south. With nineteen men and one hundred dogs on board, there was more than enough to do.

Christmas came, and the New Year went. *Fram* rounded the Cape of Good Hope, and followed her easting down. She sailed through the pack ice and icebergs of the Ross Sea, and ended her voyage at the Bay of Whales, on the Ross Ice Shelf, or the Great Ice Barrier, as it then was known, at 78°38′ South, on the edge of the Antarctic continent. On the 15th January 1911, Amundsen noted in his diary that Lt. Nilsen had

> worked out the distance sailed from Norway. It is 15,938 nautical miles, and had been estimated at 16,000. That was not bad. We had calculated on being at our field of work on the 15th January. We lay to yesterday – the 14th!

About two miles from the edge of the ice, Amundsen found a suitable site on which to build his hut, and establish his base. Framheim, it was called, "The home of *Fram*."

On the 10th February, Amundsen led some of his men out on the first of three journeys to lay depots for the following season. He had to pioneer a route through completely unexplored terrain.

> The dogs pull magnificently [he wrote in his diary]. Cannot understand what the English mean when they say that dogs cannot be used here . . . For us on skis it was the most magnificent going.

In the course of a few days, Amundsen had demythologized Antarctic travel. It *was*, after all, only ski racing writ large. By the 11th April, when the third depot journey ended, three tons of supplies had been carried out along the road to the Pole. There was a depot every degree of latitude as far as 82° South.

*Fram*, meanwhile, had sailed back to civilization. On the 21st April, the sun disappeared for the winter. Amundsen was completely isolated with eight companions, until *Fram* returned. There was no time for boredom. The depot journeys had exposed considerable deficiencies in equipment, and the long, dark polar winter seemed all too short for vital alterations.

On the 24th August, the sun returned. All winter, Amundsen had been plagued by thought of Scott. From everything he had heard, Scott was a grotesquely incompetent polar traveller; nonetheless underestimating a rival was a recipe for disaster. Amundsen desperately wanted an early start, and on the 8th September set off for the Pole.

It was too early in the season. On the 16th September, he was back at Framheim, defeated by temperatures of −50°C. Dogs had died of cold; men were frostbitten. "Many have criticized our early departure," Amundsen tellingly remarked, and one of them, Hjalmar Johansen, quarrelled with him. It was, said Amundsen, "a sad end to our wonderful unity".

In an uneasy atmosphere, they waited for warmer weather. Amundsen profited by the delay to eradicate deficiencies revealed by the abortive start. On the 20th October, delayed at the last moment by fog and gales, he finally set off. It was almost an anti-climax. The men moving with deceptive ease on ski, the dogs pattering unconcernedly over the snow, suggested some ski tour in the Norwegian mountains instead of the opening of an epic journey of exploration.

With him, Amundsen had four men and fifty-four dogs. Helmer Hanssen, having learned from the Eskimos on the North West Passage, was the leading dog driver. Another consummate dog driver was Sverre Hassel, who had spent four years in the Arctic, on another expedition in the *Fram*. Olav Bjaaland was loping along as if he were in some ski race at home. The fifth man was Oscar Wisting, a petty officer in the Norwegian navy. Neither he nor Bjaaland had driven dogs before joining Amundsen.

By the 1st November, Amundsen was leaving his depot at 81°S. Did he but know it, Scott was only then starting from his base at McMurdo Sound, two hundred miles behind. Of more immediate concern, that same day Amundsen lost his way in a fog, and stumbled into a crevassed part of the Ross Ice Shelf. He escaped without injury to man or dog. Without further setback, he ski'd on, at a steady three nautical miles (5.5 kilometres) per hour until, on the 17th November, 400 miles from Framheim, he came to the end of the great snow plain of the Ross Ice Shelf, and reached the foot of the Transantarctic Mountains.

Amundsen was not only racing against an unseen rival; he was pioneering a route through unexplored country. He had discovered the snow clad mountain range looming up ahead, and now he had to find a way to the heights. He simply drove on due south, to be confronted by a glacier, miles from shore to shore, with "terribly chaotic crevasses", as he put it. "Enormous blocks of ice, mighty abysses and wide crevasses blocked the way everywhere." He subsequently called this monster the Axel Heiberg Glacier, after one of his Norwegian backers. There was no time to find a way round. He now had forty-two dogs left. He drove them, and himself and his men, with four sledges each carrying almost half a ton, straight through the ice falls. On the 21st November, he laconically recorded:

> We won through. We are lying on the [polar] plateau at an altitude of 10,000 ft . . . The dogs – 24 of our brave comrades – received a bitter reward . . . On arrival . . . they were shot . . . The 18 best remained . . . It was a sheer marvel what those dogs accomplished . . . In 4 days we have reached the plateau from the coast – 44 miles and a climb of 10,000 ft.

The place was called the Butcher's Shop, at 85°26′S, 274 miles from the Pole. Amundsen was tent bound there for four days in a blizzard. On the 26th, in desperation, he set off nonetheless, still in a storm, with supplies for two months. For nine days, he travelled blind in fog and blizzard through dangerous, crevassed, uncharted terrain. On the 4th December, at 87°S, he ran out at last into even snow, with the occasional hummocks.

The weather still continued foul, but the snow was of the best kind; powder over crust. The skiing was good. Now there were three dog teams, driven by Helmer Hanssen, in the lead, followed by Bjaaland and Wisting, with Amundsen and Hassel skiing unencumbered. Almost without knowing it, in sunshine and perfect conditions, they reached the position of the South Pole on the afternoon of the 15th December. There were no human traces anywhere in sight.

> I cannot say . . . that I stood at my life's goal [Amundsen wrote afterwards]. I believe no human being has stood so diametrically opposed to the goal of his desires as I did . . . the North Pole had attracted me since the days of my childhood, and so I found myself at the South Pole. Can anything more perverse be conceived?

After three days taking observations to make absolutely sure of their mark, Amundsen and his companions left the Pole on the 18th December. They were undoubtedly first at the South Pole, but the race would not be won until they had brought the news back to civilization, preferably before Scott.

For the return, only sixteen dogs remained. These were reorganized into two teams, which left Olav Bjaaland, to his huge relief, without dogs at last, and free to ski ahead as forerunner. This function he performed with nonchalance, as if on some ski track at home. Except for the difficulty of breathing at high altitude, and nearly missing a depot at the Devil's Glacier, there were no more setbacks. The return journey was more or less a sprint. The descent of the Axel Heiberg Glacier, which had cost such effort to climb, resolved itself into an incomparable powder snow downhill run of a few hours. On 7th January, they were down on the Ross Ice Shelf again.

They had so much food with them, and so much more in the depots laid along their course that, in Amundsen's words, they were "living among the fleshpots of Egypt. It's just a matter now of eating as much as possible to lighten our sledges." In Eskimo sealskin clothing, they were impervious to the blizzards and cold that now intermittently assaulted them. Covering between twenty and thirty miles a day – with Bjaaland, the ski champion, ever forerunner – they raised their speed by a half, and reached Framheim on the 26th January, a fortnight earlier than expected. Men and dogs had put on weight, and were bursting with health.

So ended the longest ski race in history. Although it was a journey of exploration, Amundsen had not really been inconvenienced more than he would have been on a mountain tour at home. *Fram* had already arrived. On the 30th January, the expedition embarked, and on the 7th March, returned to civilization at Hobart, Tasmania. Amundsen had got through first with the news, and victory was complete.

On one level, it was a triumph of forethought, technical preparation, and learning what the Eskimos had to teach about survival in a polar environment. There had been one ironic hitch, however. Amundsen's camera, a large, fairly sophisticated model, proved to have been damaged. When the films from the polar journey were developed at Hobart, most proved to have been ruined.

On the way to the Pole, each man had been allowed two kilos of personal possessions. Olav Bjaaland alone had thought to bring his camera; a folding pocket Kodak, as it happened. Without that, there would have been no pictures at the Pole. Thus it was that the photographic record of the last great journey of terrestrial discovery depended on snapshots, taken in the spirit of a holidaymaker who wanted to bring home a few mementoes.

Midwinter 1898: *Belgica* (see Introduction pp. 8–9) beset in the Bellingshausen Sea. This photograph was taken by Dr F. A. Cook, using magnesium powder flashlights. *Belgica* drifted with the pack ice as far as 71°35′S before breaking free in March, 1899.

This slide symbolized the formative experience of Amundsen's life. A few months before it was taken, he had joined Dr Cook on Brabant Island for the first recorded Antarctic sledge journey. Amundsen's diary reads:

> The Doctor, the experienced polar explorer, goes ahead, I follow . . . there are many small things one can learn [from] such a thoroughly practical polar explorer . . . In his contact with the North Greenland Eskimos, and in his profound study of everything concerning polar life, he has, without doubt greater insight in these matters than most men in the field . . . He gives [advice] in a likable and tactful manner; not with fuss or noise.

All through the winter, Amundsen practised skiing over the pack ice; even when he was sick with scurvy. The disease swept through the ship. One man died.

Scurvy is acute vitamin C deficiency. Vitamins had not yet been discovered, but Dr Cook belonged to a minority that correctly considered scurvy a deficiency disease. On *Belgica*, he associated it with tinned food. He treated it by feeding his patients with fresh penguin meat.

> I am getting better every day [Amundsen wrote]. I can now give some good advice as a result of this experience . . . Try to eat as much fresh meat as possible.

That was the enduring lesson of the whole expedition.

*Fram* undergoing her refit in the naval dockyard at Horten, on the Oslo Fjord in 1909. She was originally built in 1892 for Fridtjof Nansen's Arctic expedition of 1893–6. Her designer was Colin Archer, a Norwegian of Scots extraction, who pioneered the modern lifeboat.

Nansen had deliberately frozen *Fram* in, to drift across the Arctic with the pack. She was specially constructed to withstand the pressure of the pack ice. Massively built of oak, spruce and greenheart, she had round contours, to deny the ice a grip, and rise to a squeeze.

After Nansen's drift, *Fram* was used on a second Norwegian expedition to the Canadian Arctic in 1898–1902, led by Otto Sverdrup, who had been captain of the ship under Nansen. This expedition perfected the Norwegian technique that Amundsen adopted of running dogs with men on ski. Sverdrup discovered 100,000 square miles of unknown territory. Three of his men: Sverre Hassel, Jakob Nødtvedt, the second engineer, and Adolf Henrik Lindstrøm, joined Amundsen for his new expedition. This, Amundsen was always careful to call "The *third* voyage of the *Fram*". Even in 1909, only a wooden ship was strong and elastic enough to handle polar ice.

*Fram* was originally a wet ship. For the new expedition, her bows were raised, giving extra space below decks. Also, she was rerigged as a tops'l schooner. Mainly, this was for economy of hands. The sails were mostly worked from the deck, and the ship could be run with a small crew.

2nd June, 1910: Royal visit to *Fram*. In the foreground King Haakon VII of Norway (left) and Amundsen. To the left of the King, his consort, Queen Maud. To the right of Amundsen, Thorvald Nilsen, *Fram*'s captain and, partially obscured by the Queen, Fridtjof Nansen. The background is the waterfront of Christiania (now Oslo).

The King and Queen had opened the public subscription list for the expedition with a gift of 30,000 kroner.

King Haakon and Amundsen were both national symbols. A Danish prince, the King had been called to the throne when Norway obtained its independence from Sweden in 1905. He was the first sovereign of an independent Norway for almost six hundred years. Amundsen had raised Norwegian prestige by attaining the North West Passage.

When this picture was taken, Amundsen had already decided to turn south, but was compelled to keep it secret, even from the King and Queen. In another context, he talked about having "assumed my most bland and innocent expression". This was the strain under which he had to labour for a year.

In the end, when Amundsen announced his change of plan, he made sure that King Haakon was amongst the first to know. He asked an intermediary to deliver a letter to Nansen,

and one of similar content to the King, simultaneously. In this way, both receive the message *at the same moment*. It means much to me that this is done.

Amundsen bidding farewell to the Norwegian King and Queen after their visit to *Fram*. Amundsen is standing outboard, touching his cap. Next to him is King Haakon, followed by Queen Maud. The figure behind Queen Maud, touching his cap, is Nansen.

> We were warned in advance of Their Majesties' arrival [as Amundsen put it] and we tried as best we could to bring a little order into the chaos on board. I am not sure whether we had much luck.

> Stowing ship was just coming to an end. It was a complex process, which had taken more than a month. *Fram* had to be loaded in such a way that, when she reached the ice, every single item was available in the correct order.

Each member of the landing party, for example, had eight sets of clothing: rainwear, working clothes, tropical rig and cold weather garments for the voyage; working clothes for the base on shore, skiing outfits for normal Antarctic weather, sealskin garments from Northern Greenland for colder conditions, and Netsilik reindeer fur clothing, for the very worst conceivable cold.

On the 3rd June 1910, the day after this picture was taken, *Fram* sailed down the fjord to Amundsen's home, there to take on the rest of her cargo, embark her crew, and depart.

*Fram*, anchored outside Amundsen's home, in Bundefjord, an inlet of the Oslo Fjord, early June 1910.
Amundsen is standing at the end of his estate, on the banks
of the fjord, with Pan, a St Bernard, his favourite dog.

It was here that Amundsen's secret first seriously came
under threat. For his base in Antarctica, he had ordered
a prefabricated wooden hut. In his garden, by the shore
(to the right of this picture), he arranged its trial assembly.
He rather lamely called it an "observation house" for the
pack ice.

> The more experienced members of the expedition obviously
> brooded over . . . this "observation house" [Amundsen wrote].
> "I can just about understand that you want to be warm and
> comfortable when you observe," said Helmer Hanssen, "but
> why you need oilcloth on the table, I cannot grasp."

About three months before this picture was taken, Scott
tried to make an appointment to discuss simultaneous
magnetic observations. Amundsen knew he was in Norway
to test motor sledges he was having designed for the
Antarctic. He refused to answer the telephone, and managed to avoid meeting Scott altogether.

At the age of thirty-eight, Amundsen was still un-
married. He lived in a large wooden house, like a Swiss
chalet, with Betty, his old nurse, as housekeeper. In the
days before departure, however, he was not alone. Some
members of his expedition were staying with him to cope
with last minute preparations. There was constant traffic
from ship to shore.

On the 6th June, Amundsen gave a little farewell party
for all his companions in the garden, with this view of
*Fram*. Late in the evening, they all went on board. "Sailed
at midnight," Amundsen wrote on the first page of his
diary, repeating exactly the words with which he had
opened his diary for the North West Passage, seven years
before. "Still and clear," he continued. "A wonderful
summer's night."

He had chosen the hour to slip away as quietly as
possible. Also, the 7th June was the Norwegian Independence Day.

*Fram* first spent a month on a preliminary cruise in the
North Atlantic to test crew and ship. Then she went to
Kristiansand on the south coast of Norway to pick up the
dogs, which had been delivered there from Greenland.

Meanwhile, Amundsen was still short of 150,000 kroner.
Ten days before departure, "Don Pedro" Christopherson,
a Norwegian living in Argentina, offered free supplies if
*Fram* touched at Montevideo or Buenos Aires. Creditors
were still lined up in Norway; but the future now seemed
considerably less bleak. It was, he wrote in his diary for
the 9th August,

> a wonderful feeling to be able to cast off and head for our goal
> at last. After taking our 97 dogs on board this afternoon, we
> weighed anchor and stood out [to sea] at 8.30. Still and clear.
> Warm as the finest summer's day . . . Heading for the Channel.
> All well.

*Left*] *Fram* off the Christiania (Oslo) waterfront, looking aft. Amundsen is standing nearest the mast. Next to him, rolled chart in hand, is *Fram*'s captain, Thorvald Nilsen. The foreground figure is Andreas Beck, *Fram*'s ice pilot. Although he did not yet know it, he was to navigate through the pack ice guarding the entrance to the Ross Sea. The fate of the expedition might depend on his skill.

*Above*] Amundsen, Pan and friends on his estate at Bundefjord. Amundsen was inordinately fond of animals and, as he said, could never understand anyone who killed living creatures for pleasure. Yet the plan he had worked out for reaching the South Pole required sledge dogs to be put down in cold blood as their usefulness ended. In Amundsen's own words: "Having embarked on this record hunt, at all costs, we had to be first. Everything had to be subordinated to that end."

Thorvald Nilsen rating the ship's chronometers at Madeira. He is using a sextant and artificial horizon (a tray of mercury) to observe the sun's altitude. This was his last opportunity to check the chronometers before the long voyage to the Antarctic. There was no wireless on board, and hence no possibility of time checks along the way.

Under the original plan, *Fram* was to enter the Arctic through the Bering Strait. Since the Panama Canal was not yet open, that meant sailing by way of Cape Horn. In fact, she was going to the Antarctic round the Cape of Good Hope. As far as Madeira, it was impossible to tell where she was really heading. Afterwards, the paths diverged. That was why Amundsen chose Madeira to disclose his secret to his men, and tell them he was going south, instead of north.

It was from Madeira that Amundsen's brother, Leon, took back post to be delivered after he had announced the change of plan. That was on 1st October, by when *Fram* was well out to sea, and beyond all possibility of recall.

From Madeira, Leon had a letter from his brother to Fridtjof Nansen, explaining that he had decided to "take part in the contest" for the South Pole:

> I have often wished that Scott could have learned of my decision, so that it would not seem as if I wanted to sneak down there without his knowledge in order to forestall him: but I have not dared to make any kind of announcement, for fear of being stopped.

Leon, on behalf of his brother, now cabled Scott in Melbourne: "Beg leave to inform you Fram proceeding Antarctic. Amundsen." In his letter to Nansen, Amundsen wrote that

> it is my intention not to dog the Englishmen's footsteps. They have naturally the first right. We must make do with what they discard.

Scott was making for his and Shackleton's old base on Ross Island in McMurdo Sound, at the south western corner of the Ross Sea. Amundsen was heading for the Bay of Whales, on the Ross Ice Shelf, some 400 miles to the east. This was a formation which Shackleton had seen, and named, in 1908, but which he rejected as a base for fear of the ice calving under his feet and sending him out to sea. Amundsen nonetheless decided to land there:

> I had given this formation . . . a special study, and came to the conclusion that what today is known as the Bay of Whales is nothing else than the selfsame bay [previously] observed . . . admittedly with a number of big changes, but nonetheless the same. For 70 years [it had] remained in the same place.

Besides, at the Bay of Whales, Amundsen would be a whole degree, or sixty miles, closer to the Pole than Scott at McMurdo Sound.

But the dogs were the key to the enterprise.

"Our four-footed companions," Amundsen called his dogs. "'Kamilla' had 4 pups during the night," he recorded at the end of August. "All doing well. Kept two dogs, but [destroyed] the bitches." Having embarked with ninety-seven dogs, Amundsen now had ninety-nine.

This picture shows Jørgen Stubberud with Kamilla and family on the deck of *Fram* in the trade winds. Stubberud was a carpenter who had built the hut for Amundsen's Antarctic base. Amundsen brought him along to be absolutely certain of the correct assembly.

There were ten bitches on board, so that, as Amundsen put it,

> we had every right to expect an increase in numbers during the voyage south. [A] "happy event" [might] seem of little significance, but for us, living in circumstances where the one day was very like the next, it was more than enough to be the object of the greatest interest.

Life on board revolved round the dogs. *Fram* was like a floating kennel. Everybody understood that the fortunes of the expedition stood or fell with the dogs. They appeared constantly in Amundsen's diary.

The dogs, incidentally, at one point threatened Amundsen's secret. Nansen, for one, was puzzled by their presence on board. Why go to all the trouble of taking the dogs through the tropics, if the Arctic was their destination? The logical procedure was surely to pick them up in Alaska. Somehow, Amundsen disarmed these suspicions; but it was a near thing.

"The dogs, ah, the dogs," Amundsen apostrophized in his diary. *Fram*'s voyage south was punctuated by whelping, which inspired Amundsen to quote a Norwegian sea chanty:

> *Virgins are sacred ashore,*
> *May not come on board,*
> *But Freia, she fell for temptation.*

In this picture, Lt. Kristian Prestrud (left) and Karenius Olsen (right), *Fram*'s cook, are feeding pups some time after leaving Madeira.

Prestrud was a navigational specialist, asked by Amundsen to devise a simple and accurate method of navigation on the polar journey. In the snows, without landmarks, navigation was very similar to that at sea.

The figure half hidden by a stanchion is Jakob Nødtvedt, *Fram*'s second engineer. He had set up a forge on deck, and was making equipment, including patent catches for dog harnesses and ski bindings. Amundsen mistrusted ordinary commercial products.

> Just as well we don't take anything on trust [he wrote]. If we are to win, not a trouser button must be missing.

"Men and dogs," he went on, "are enjoying themselves beyond all expectations."

> Nødtvedt has his forge next to a kennel . . . with 4 . . . puppies. "They are funny to watch," says N. "When they have drunk milk and are wet around the muzzle, they lick each other in the most affectionate way. But, when the muzzles are licked dry, with nothing more to get, then they start fighting."

"Everybody," says Amundsen, "is looking after their dogs splendidly." Of course self interest was involved. Upon the wellbeing of the dogs depended the outcome of the expedition.

From Amundsen's diary for the Sunday, 2nd October:

> The southerly breeze continues. Went about at midday, and are now sailing SE. Today we had our equator dinner, even although we were a few degrees north. We did not have time to waste a weekday on that kind of nonsense.

Amundsen meant the ceremony of "crossing the line", when those who had not yet crossed the Equator, had to submit to an initiation, in which Father Neptune played a leading and not exactly a considerate rôle.

> After a good dinner [Amundsen continued], coffee and liqueurs were served on deck, decorated for the occasion with flags. Gjertsen appeared as a dancer, performing admirably. Indeed, he looked so convincing in a little, short, flowered dress made of gauze – and in dark, false curls – that certain members of the expedition played along with the deception and made the obvious approaches. Thereafter, Nilsen played the part of a comedian. A better performance would be difficult to imagine. Both turns were warmly applauded.

"We care for our dogs like little children," Amundsen wrote, as *Fram* entered the doldrums.

> Dogs have rarely had such care . . . Everyone is anxious to busy himself with them. [Oscar] Wisting however wins first prize. He is tireless, and always on the go.

This picture shows Wisting feeding a pup while the mother looks on. Amundsen noted that Thorvald Nilsen, the ship's captain,

> had assumed supervision of all maternity establishments. Every afternoon at 3.15, he brings milk and pudding round to all the women who have just had their babies.

A bitch called Kaisa disrupted the idyll:

> During the night we lost . . . a beautiful big pup belonging to "Kaisa" . . . She has always seemed indifferent to her offspring. This morning we found bloodstains [on the deck]. When Kaisa – normally a big eater – refused her food, we concluded that she had eaten up the youngster.

Amundsen chronicled the dogs' routine:

> At 9 a.m., they have stockfish 5 times weekly and, twice, stockfish boiled together with tallow and maize. They like both, but the latter is their favourite dish. 4 to 5 p.m., they have stockfish again. Their ration is ½ kilo stockfish daily.

Stubberud with two of his favourites on board *Fram*. "These dogs," as Amundsen put it, "are wonderful."

We grow fonder and fonder of them every day. And the affection is mutual. They howl with pleasure when they see us.

Amundsen believed that the critical part would not be the actual polar journey, but getting the dogs safe and sound through the tropics. Antibiotics did not yet exist, and epidemic disease was the great fear. On the 1st October, just before crossing the Equator, Amundsen was relieved to observe:

State of health good, both among people and dogs. Water is our weak point . . . The dogs have 2 litres each daily, and we 19 men must manage with 50 litres altogether. In this way, we will have water for . . . 4 months.

Of himself, Amundsen recorded:

I have now begun to train for the southern excursion. Stopped smoking on the 15th [September] and won't taste tobacco again until the work is done.

But the diary during the voyage never strayed far from the dogs:

To look after all our children we had to work systematically. Each dog has a little metal tag with his name. Then the dogs have been distributed among 8 of us, so that each man has to care for about 12 . . . Each man had to name his dogs, but a lot of names are needed for 100 dogs . . . As we grew familiar with them, we have rearranged the groups so that those who knew each other were reunited.

Into the commentary on daily events, extraneous thoughts occasionally intruded; for example on the 30th September:

The publication at home of my South Pole plans is now approaching. I am fully aware of the boldness of the plan and the great responsibility that rests on me. With the help of my able companions, I will manage. God help us.

Martin Rønne, *Fram*'s sailmaker, somewhat doubtfully holding what he called a "beast". He did not quite approve of dogs on board. On the other hand, he was a vital craftsman, doing all the sewing, from duffel bags to boots. "Work on polar equipment is carried on with determination, despite violent rolling and difficult conditions," Amundsen noted on the 1st November.

> Today Rønne has cut out a sledging tent in the chart-house, and tacked it together . . . [Ludwig] Hansen does the finest tinsmith's work and Nødtvedt forges the strangest things up on deck in the midst of this confusion. They are sheer acrobats, all three. I really do admire them.

Hansen was making paraffin tins for the polar journey. They were specially designed, with silver soldered seams to avoid the leakage that had bedevilled previous expeditions. Meanwhile, Olav Bjaaland, the expedition's best skier, and a skilled carpenter into the bargain, was preparing sledges, ski and bindings. "Everything," Amundsen reiterated, "will have to be tip-top."

To keep the ship clean, and the dogs comfortable, loose boards were laid on joists over the whole deck, forming a cover, with a space in between. This false deck, as Amundsen put it,

> has been wonderful. All water . . . runs underneath the dogs, who are thus always dry. Decks are washed down twice daily. Twice weekly, the loose boards are removed, and the deck underneath washed down. Furthermore, laths have been nailed to the loose boards so that the animals have something to grip on when the ship rolls.

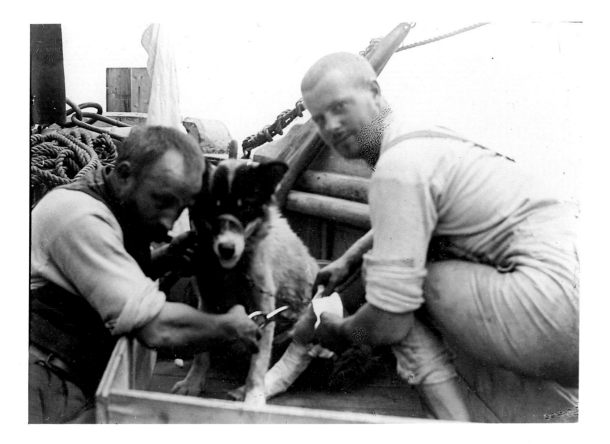

Soon after passing the Equator, a dog called Isak broke his leg on board. Wisting (left) and F. H. Gjertsen (right), *Fram*'s second mate, set the bone.

> We hope it will grow together [Amundsen wrote]. We cannot afford to lose this dog, who is both big and good-tempered . . . Many of our dogs . . . are suffering . . . from swollen paws and claws are falling off [because] their claws are not worn down on the deck, and grow unchecked . . . We must try to cut their claws.

Then the dogs started to grow thin and lose condition. They were cured with extra fat, mainly with butter from the crew's rations. There was no other sickness among the dogs.

For two months, the dogs were each tethered, unable to move about. Finally, on the 2nd October, they were tentatively let loose, all 112, including pups. The adults were muzzled and, in Amundsen's words:

There were many violent encounters, but without any ill effects, since they absolutely could not injure each other . . . They looked quite sheepish when they grasped their own helplessness.

Amundsen was soon writing that, "The dogs are having halcyon days now. They are free day and night and can fight when they wish." Finally, at the end of October, when they seemed to have got the fighting out of their system, they were successfully let loose without muzzles. By then they were in the Roaring Forties but, as Amundsen put it, the dogs

> have got their sea legs . . . They manage the pitching and tossing brilliantly. They are better than us.

*Fram*'s foredeck in the Trade Winds (*left*), taken from the bowsprit. *Fram*, said Amundsen,

> had a leak of an unpleasant kind. It is so high that water enters the 'tween decks, where we have our provisions, and destroys them. *Fram* is like a sieve above the waterline, but her hull is good.

When *Fram* was under sail alone, she had to be pumped out by hand. This took about an hour each day. It was time that Amundsen could ill afford, since every minute seemed to count in getting ready for the Antarctic. On the 13th October, for example, he recorded that

> work on the dog harnesses was started. The yokes are to be covered with cloth, so that they will not wear out too quickly. Besides, we will sew a complete new set of traces.

Next day he wrote:

> I have done a lot of developing today. The cinematograph pictures turned out really well. So did my films. The others' results were mixed.

In warm latitudes, an awning was rigged on *Fram*'s deck for the dogs. It appears in the picture on the left and, above, the dogs are lying in its shade. Although adapted to polar conditions, they were untroubled by the heat, provided they were protected from the direct rays of the sun. Water, however, was running low, and they could not have all they wanted. By the end of October, the original ninety-seven dogs had increased to 118.

"Many of us have taken photographs of various seas," Amundsen wrote.

> We want to expose the humbug often involved in photographing a sea so as to appear much worse than it really is.

This picture may be misleading, since *Fram*, to quote the diary of Hjalmar Johansen,

> rolls day and night without respite . . . At every meal, we have to lash our chairs to the deck . . . not a moment's peace since we left Norway except for the 2–3 days at Madeira.

*Fram* had been designed for the pack ice. She was round-bottomed, to avoid being crushed, but in a seaway this made her heel over to the slightest swell. Nonetheless, Amundsen decided that "a finer seaboat does not exist." On the 11th November, he recorded a south westerly storm:

> The sea rose up to a fairly noticeable height. Some [waves] reached the maximum on the scale – 10 metres high. But – how wonderfully [*Fram*] takes them. As long as one is careful to keep her stern towards these bouncers, one would not know that one was at sea . . . She lurches all right, but not a drop of water does she take on board.

When Amundsen wrote this, he was rounding the Cape, three hundred miles out to sea. It was two months since he had seen land, but he still wanted to give civilization a wide berth:

> I have . . . no desire to make contact with people now. Everybody will want to write home, and the papers will naturally have a lot to say.

Taking in the tops'l; on *Fram*, notably unpleasant, since she was undermanned. Of the nineteen men on board, eight were concentrating on preparations for the polar journey. Working the ship was cut to a minimum. It might take an hour to furl the tops'l.

Luckily, this was not very often. For lack of funds, Amundsen had to make do with clumsy old gear aloft. *Fram* was rigged as a schooner, and most of the time was under her fore-and-aft sails alone. These were worked from the deck, and needed few hands.

Besides, *Fram* had auxiliary engines. Appearances were deceptive. She looked like a romantic harkback to the age of sail; perhaps with a touch of a pirate ship. In fact, she was a revolutionary vessel. In her engine room, she had the third diesel motor ever fitted to an ocean going ship. This was the historic first long voyage under diesel power.

Amundsen had made the experiment because oil was cleaner than coal, and gave a greater range. Also, he would have instant power exactly when required. In the doldrums, he wrote:

> The motor is brilliant beyond words. [It runs] day after day without trouble . . . oil consumption is less than calculated; which is just as well, because winds have been light.

To economize fuel, sail was set whenever possible. In Amundsen's own words:

> I have given orders to start [the motor] when our speed falls below 5 knots.

This was necessary to keep up with his timetable.

Martin Rønne (left) and Adolf Henrik Lindstrøm (right) in the Roaring Forties with an albatross the latter had caught. The albatross, said Amundsen, was

> fished up with a hook made of a pin. The line was ordinary black cotton. How odd that such a big bird can be caught with such weak tackle. But it must be the pain that forces it to fall down obediently and offer no resistance.

Lindstrøm removed the skin from the albatross, and added it to the ornithological collection he was making for a Christiania museum. Amundsen bitterly remarked that it would "keep those children in the assembly happy". He meant the Norwegian politicians who had grudgingly, in his view, given him the minimum of grants for his expedition.

By training, Lindstrøm was a ship's cook. He came from Hammerfest, in northern Norway, and had sailed mostly on sealers in the Arctic. He had been with Amundsen before, on *Gjøa*, on the North West Passage. Now, on *Fram*, in Amundsen's words,

> Lindstrøm has resumed his old position on *Gjøa* – steward, and zoologist. He is just the same as before; tireless in his work, happy and content at all times.

Amundsen returned to the theme. Lindstrøm was

> an extraordinary person. He is now both ship's engineer and steward. I have no idea when he sleeps, since he is to be seen at all hours of the day and night.

The dogs had the run of the ship. "The most attractive place . . . is the bridge," Amundsen indulgently remarked.

In a storm they pack themselves together [there] – up to 50 at a time – for mutual support. Nonetheless there are many battles after every big lurch . . . Poor devils . . . they take the shock as a personal affront.

The Eskimo dog nonetheless was

extraordinarily intelligent. I have recently started chasing my dogs off the bridge at 6 a.m., in order to clean up . . . At eight bells, I allow them back. Once was enough for them to associate these 8 strokes of the bell with permission to return. Next morning they rushed up as one man at 8 bells.

Amundsen noted on the 12th November that the dogs were

also allowed to use the chart-house. At night, up to 20 will pack themselves in. Inside, they are mostly peaceful. Last night, however, a battle took place because there were two rivals for the desk.

"In naming our many dogs," Amundsen ironically added, "we have naturally not omitted Peary and – Cook."

In the stormy Southern Ocean, as *Fram* was approaching Antarctica, a dog occasionally fell overboard. Amundsen wrote about a "melancholy loss" when this happened to one called Maren. She was

a small, intelligent bitch. She was very fond of me and followed me everywhere. Her most hated rival for my favour was another little red-haired bitch, Tinka. They always fought over which would be the first to say "Good morning" to me when I came topsides.

Dogs sunning themselves on the foredeck of *Fram*, after passing through the tropics safe and sound. Amundsen considered this the crisis of the whole expedition. If the dogs survived the heat, and disease was kept at bay then he felt, barring accidents, he would win the race for the South Pole.

In the event, Amundsen suffered more than the dogs. He described how he took photographs on deck one morning in the tropics, clad in a light vest:

> In the evening, I felt how the sun had scorched my back all the way down to the waist. [For] two nights, I have found it difficult to lie down.

In this picture, the false deck for washing down can be clearly seen. Nonetheless, with over one hundred dogs on board, it was impossible to keep the ship absolutely clean. Wisting made the point:

> Working sails in the dark, [one heard] fairly unambiguous expressions about dogs on a ship, when ropes slid too easily through fingers well greased with "soft soap".

Rønne maintained his armed neutrality towards man's best friend. Amundsen noted on the 5th November, as *Fram* was making her Easting down, past the Cape of Good Hope:

the water used for the dogs now comes from a [rusty] iron tank . . . The water therefore contains a lot of rust . . . which has noticeably affected the dogs' stools . . . Recently there was talk of [the magnetic compass] deviation changing with surprising speed . . . "What do you expect?" said Rønne. "The dogs are shitting iron all over the place."

*Above]* *Fram's* navigators "shooting the sun". F. H. Gjertsen (left), Thorvald Nilsen, Kristian Prestrud, respectively second mate, captain, and first mate on the outward voyage, pose with their sextants.

On the 1st December Amundsen wrote in his diary:

I have today selected the members of the wintering party: Kr. Prestrud, Hj. Johansen, Sv. Hassel, Ad. Lindstrøm, H. Hanssen, O. Wisting, Olav Bjaaland and J. Stubberud. With myself, we will be 9. Originally, this party was to consist of 10 participants, but since there were only 19 on board, I find it only fair that the ship has 10.

Almost everyone, in fact, wanted to go ashore.

*Fram* had passed the 70th meridian East, and was half way across the Indian Ocean. She had been continuously at sea now for almost three months. More than a month of the voyage remained. Nonetheless, on the 5th December, in Amundsen's own words:

The plan for our work on arrival at the Barrier [Ross Ice Shelf] was posted in the chart-house today. N. [Nilsen] has a splendid grasp of the distribution of work, and he is the author of the plan. I have accepted every word; it is perfection itself.

A feeling of journey's end was in the air. On the 27th December, Amundsen recorded

Thick fog most of the day . . . In the afternoon, saw a large flock of penguins (small) in the sea. They were heading due South – Both fog and penguins are distinct signs that we are not far from the ice.

*Fram* crossed the Antarctic Circle in the evening of the 2nd January 1911. "We have now found the sea free of ice further South than anyone else," Amundsen wrote that day. "But – we will meet it in the end."

It happened the following day, and this picture shows the view from the deck. The figures on the ice are some of *Fram's* crew flensing a seal. Amundsen's diary reads:

The ice through which we have gone lies in streams with broad, open leads in between [with] a few eroded icebergs. We have seen no large icebergs. An occasional seal has been seen here and there. In those cases, we stop and take it . . . It has been a red letter day for all of us. For dinner we had steak – the finest and tenderest meat . . . The dogs have done just as well. For dinner they had each their huge piece of meat, about 2 kilos, together with a large piece of skin with blubber. To begin with, they did not really grasp the change from stockfish to fresh seal meat – but it did not take them

long . . . I estimate that the . . . heaviest seal we caught weighs about 500 kilos. Not many of those fellows will be needed to feed the dogs during the winter.

On the 5th January, Amundsen noted that

The Midnight Sun was visible for the first time today. It was a wonderful sight on this beautiful evening. It is almost calm; just a breath of wind from the S.E. . . .

Who can describe the wonderful feeling of wellbeing that has enveloped us here in the calm waters among the ice, with plenty of fresh water – or rather fresh ice – and fine, fresh meat, after 4 months' unending, intolerable pitching and tossing? I believe that hardly anyone who has not experienced this, can properly understand to what degree we appreciate the change.

This pleasure was short lived. After little more than three days, *Fram* ran out of the pack ice, and, once more, as Amundsen put it, "the swell is heavy, and everything

is familiar." With remarkable ease, *Fram* had cleared the belt of ice guarding the Ross Sea. It was the fastest passage of the ice yet. Partly, this was due to Amundsen's meticulous study of previous voyages. Much was also due to Beck, the ice pilot, who found a way through, when *Fram* seemed in danger of being stopped. Now, she was rolling over the open waters of the Ross Sea.

> We are forging ahead under full sail and with the engine running as well, and doing 6–7 knots. If we carry on like this, the remaining 500 miles will soon be but a memory. We are all longing to start our work down there.

Amundsen's thoughts were never far from the dogs:

> I can safely say that the animals love us. It is not only on account of the copious food they have always received, but also – indeed especially, I believe – because of loving care. With my own eyes I have seen men saving some of their own dinner portions to give their dogs when they showed signs of illness; only because they were so fond of them. Take note, ladies and gentlemen who profess kindness to animals.

Criticism about the use of dogs still rankled. In any case, Amundsen could not quite hide from himself the fact that his plans for reaching the South Pole involved putting dogs down when they were no longer needed, and feeding them to the survivors.

The last of the ice, before entering the Ross Sea. *Fram* has stopped, and sent a boat away to shoot seal basking on this floe. In Amundsen's words:

> We are gorging ourselves with fresh [seal] meat, we like it so much. But then Lindstrøm is a past master in cooking it.

Amundsen was self-confessedly a gourmet, but gastronomy was now hardly his main concern. He had been without fresh food for four months. The danger of scurvy was not entirely academic. Plenty of fresh, underdone meat would keep it at bay. Experiments a few years before in Amundsen's native Christiania had proved scurvy to be a deficiency disease.

Although dogs do not suffer from scurvy, it was clear that they needed fresh meat for good health. "I will try and feed them up properly, before they get into harness down there," Amundsen wrote as he entered the pack ice, and the first seal were shot. For better or worse, dogs change condition quickly. Within a very few days, Amundsen was writing that

> The dogs have overeaten. [Sometimes] they cannot manage their meat ration. They are now, almost without exception, all big, round and fat. I dare say they are at the top of their power and appetite for life, and ready to do good work.

*Fram*'s saloon, with Christmas decorations. (The photographs over the piano are of King Haakon and Queen Maud of Norway.) On the 19th October, Amundsen noted that he was

> sorting Christmas presents . . . – 300–400 – and divided them over 5–6 years. We take one year's supply [ashore].

The stock was intended for the original Arctic drift. From Amundsen's diary for Christmas Eve:

> We were all invited to dinner in the forward saloon [which] was beautifully decorated. Lt. Nilsen was responsible for the decorations, with my assistance . . . Delightful little coloured lanterns (16 in all) . . . gave a pleasant illumination, and a nice ambience . . . I had the gramophone suspended in gimbals in my cabin. The guests arrived at 5 p.m., and when all had taken their places . . . "Holy Night, Silent Night", burst out, sung by Herold. Heavens, what a ceremony – what an effect. One had to be made of more than steel not to feel the tears coming. The gramophone was completely hidden. No one expected it . . . And then we . . . ate, drank, and enjoyed ourselves . . . After dinner we went to the after saloon, where coffee was served . . . Thereafter we returned to the forward saloon, where the Christmas tree . . . decorated by Lindstrøm, awaited us. Here we were enriched by many splendid presents. This wonderful party finished at 11 p.m. – The wind was fairly light, and did not disturb the festivities. This Christmas Eve will always live in the memory of the *Fram* men. And many warm thanks were sent home to those who had thought of us with gifts.

Antarctica at last: *Fram* alongside at the Bay of Whales, 15th January 1911. She had arrived two days earlier, after four months continually at sea. Unloading the ship and dog driving have just begun. Amundsen's diary reads:

It took some time before [the] animals . . . understood that the quiet, lazy life on board was now over, and that a new era of work and drudgery lay ahead. To begin with, they really seemed somewhat doubtful. But after having changed their positions in the traces, things went – brilliantly. Naturally, a spurt ended frequently in the wildest confusion. In the end, however, we managed somehow. With a little practice, things will get better. On board, when we stole a glance, we saw grinning heads above the bulwarks. They obviously thought the dogs were going to get the upper hand.

Everybody could ski, but only Amundsen, Helmer Hanssen, Hassel and Hjalmar Johansen had driven dogs before. Next day, Amundsen noted that

all dogs were landed. At the same time we drove up all supplies and equipment we dared load on the sledges the first time . . . We have had a lot of trouble with driving today. There have been hidings for the dogs; but it has been necessary to make them understand the gravity of the situation. Things will soon be better.

The first camp had been established, about a mile back from the edge of the ice, and Amundsen was anxious to move his supplies there as quickly as he could.

*Fram* lay to at the Bay of Whales in the afternoon of 13th January 1911. This picture shows her moored at the edge of the sea ice, with the cliffs of the Ross Ice Shelf – "The Barrier", as Amundsen knew it – in the background. Soon after arrival

> Prestrud, Johansen, and I went off on ski to investigate the terrain [Amundsen wrote]. The skiing was excellent, and it was good to move one's limbs again after the four months [at sea]. A few miles to the south we found a lead, which proved so difficult for a skier to cross, that I had to give up any hope of getting through with sledges in that direction . . . We turned back and arrived on board at 1 a.m.

A few hours later, *Fram*

> stood . . . along the edge of the sea ice, [and soon] arrived at the south-easterly corner of [the bay]. We moored . . . and went out to reconnoitre. This time the party consisted of Helmer Hanssen, Prestrud, Johansen, and myself . . . The weather was brilliant; sunny and warm . . . After . . . two miles the ice foot led onto the Barrier by a small, even slope; an ideal connection in other words. We continued in a south-easterly direction and after about 15 minutes reached one of the [previously observed] ridge formations on the Barrier . . . I selected a place – in a hollow, on a fine, flat foundation, about 4 miles from the . . . sea, as our future residence. Here we will build our home, and from here our work will be carried out.

"Great excitement," Amundsen wrote on the 3rd February 1911.

> When we came down to our vessel this morning, instead of our dear *Fram* alone, there were – two vessels at the ice edge. The latest arrival was a large barque – *Terra Nova*.

"To our wild excitement," wrote Wilfred Bruce, one of *Terra Nova*'s officers,

> we turned into the Bay of Whales [and] saw a ship tied up to the sea-ice. It was the "*Fram*" . . . Amundsen, Nilsen &

Prestrud lunched on board [*Terra Nova*] & were very friendly, but didn't give away very much or get much!

Amundsen found the Englishmen "extraordinarily pleasant". He did learn that *Terra Nova* had tried

> to reach King Edward Land – but without success. She was now on her way back . . . to the main base at McMurdo Sound.

Together with the rest of *Terra Nova*'s crew, Bruce was shown over *Fram*. She was "very comfortable . . . very ugly outside". Individually, said Bruce, the Norwegians

"all seemed charming men, even the perfidious Amundsen". On *Terra Nova*, when she left again, after a few hours, there were

> heavy arguments . . . about the rights & wrongs of Amundsen's party & the chances of our being able to beat them. Their experience & number of dogs seem to leave us very little.

This was the news to be conveyed to Scott at McMurdo Sound. As Bruce put it, there could be "nothing so exciting as the *Fram*'s discovery, an eruption of Erebus [the volcano at McMurdo Sound] would fall flat after that".

This picture shows skuas round the carcass of a seal near *Fram* at the Bay of Whales. "We are living in a veritable never-never land," as Amundsen put it. "Seals come to the ship, and allow themselves to be shot." He wanted his meat supply for the year ahead secured as quickly as possible. The skiing, he observed, was good.

"A lovelier sight than that I saw this morning . . . when driving my sledge down from the . . . camp, I have never seen," Amundsen wrote in his diary, a few days after landing at the Bay of Whales.

> The only pity is that I cannot describe it properly. Between Mount Nelson and Mount Rønniken – two old disturbances in the ice – there was a view which made my heart beat quickly. The outlying part of the Barrier lay on the other side of the bay, shining white, and bathed in sunshine. Below this, the water seemed black against the white wall. Nearby, lay our closest neighbour, the vertical barrier – about 100 ft. [high] and gleaming in the strangest blue colour. And in this fairy tale world lay little *Fram*, all on its own. It was insignificant in this mighty landscape.

In another entry, Amundsen returned to this theme:

> We human beings have intruded in this fairy tale landscape to wrest its secrets from it; those secrets which have been hidden for millennia.

That day, "the weather was wonderful. Brilliant sunshine, and mostly dead calm."

> The sun, the cold, and the dry air have burned us, so that we look worse than the lowest tramps. My nose, lips, jaw and forehead are just a single sore.

Men and dogs soon got used to their work. Here, sledges are moving over the sea ice at the Bay of Whales.

"The going has been good," Amundsen reported on the 18th January, three days after landing. "The sun has had a considerable effect on the [snow]. Wide, polished expanses help to keep the sledges moving."

Amundsen's first camp on the Barrier, established on the 15th January 1911, in his own words, "as a temporary residence for the dogs".

It lay 1.2 nautical miles from the ship. Here . . . in a pleasant little valley, we pitched a 16 man tent for the dog minders J. & H. [Johansen and Hassel], together with passing travellers. Round the tent we then ran a wire in the form of a triangle – each side 50m. – where our animals will be placed. We then continued our march to the place we had selected for our house. It lay only 2.2 nautical miles from the ship. In this way, our landing will be much quicker than originally planned.

Amundsen had assumed that his base would have to be ten miles inland, so that, if the Barrier calved, he would not drift out to sea on an iceberg. Having now actually seen the terrain, he was persuaded that the lesser distance was enough.

At the appointed place, we marked out the building plot – in a SE–NW direction, and pitched [another] 16 man tent for the use of Bj. & Jørg. [Olav Bjaaland and Jørgen Stubberud], who will be the builders.

On our return journey, we marked the whole route with dark blue pennants, so that it will be impossible to lose one's way. These marks have been placed at intervals of 15 paces. We were on board again at 5 p.m. – Took some photos of this first trip of ours.

Another snapshot of the first camp; now an occasional stop for the dog teams ferrying supplies from the ship to the base. Meanwhile, the hut was being built, and Amundsen's diary for the 23rd January 1911 reads:

As usual, we drove a load up before breakfast. The first run brought the remaining things for the hut, like bunks, stoves, etc. Afterwards we began carrying provisions. It is a matter of 900 packing cases . . . We have done 5 runs today, but hope to manage 6 tomorrow. [Since] each sledge load consists generally of 5 cases, [hence] 25 cases per run, [that] means 150 cases in the course of a day. In this way, we will get them all carried up quickly.

A few days later, Amundsen wrote:

6 inches of snow fell during the night. The going was bad [but] we did 6 runs and tomorrow [28th January] we will finish . . . It was a brilliant piece of work, and I cannot but admire the patience and diligence of all concerned.

The tent in the picture came from a stock scrounged from the Norwegian army. During the voyage from Madeira, Rønne had sewn groundsheets into some of them.

The mountain-like shapes in the background are mounds of ice piled up by a disturbance in the barrier.

The men only skied on the way up; on the return to the ship, they rode on the empty sledges. The object on the tripod is a cine camera or, as Amundsen called it "A Cinematograph apparatus".

Jørgen Stubberud and Olav Bjaaland, building the expedition hut. Stubberud had constructed it in Norway, of prefabricated sections. It had its trial assembly in Amundsen's garden, and was designed to be erected by two men alone. They had to dig the foundations out of snow and ice; work that "fully demonstrated their skill and determination", as Amundsen wrote on the 17th January, when the work began.

> The temperature was −7°[C.] . . . When the weather broke in the forenoon, they had already shovelled a good deal of snow from the site. But when the snow began drifting the site was immediately covered, and they had to abandon the work . . . And then [they] had an idea. With [some] planks and empty sledges, they built a wedge-shaped wall against the wind and thereby completely diverted the drift. Under its protection, they managed to dig out the site completely – very long and exhausting work.

Five days later

> The roof was on. All further work [on the hut] can thus take place – inside and cannot be inhibited by the weather.
> This afternoon, while they were working on the house, Bj. & Jørg. heard a violent noise in the ice, far away. Probably an iceberg calving, or formation of crevasses in the barrier.

Finally, on the 28th January,

> All of us, except Lindstrøm, moved into the hut this afternoon. Very fine work has been done. Within 14 days of the site being chosen, the house had been completed, and virtually all provisions landed.

The finishing touches to the hut were the chimney, and tarred paper to seal the roof. Thereupon, in Amundsen's words, "our hut was baptised and given the name 'Framheim'." This means "The home of Fram", and was obviously inspired by certain Norwegian mountain names, like Trollheim, "The home of the trolls."

> The idea [said Amundsen], was Prestrud's. We had the ship's party, or as they are called, the pirates, for a house warming.

The whole base was soon called Framheim too. It was fairly extensive. "We have now pitched 14 of the 16 man tents here," Amundsen noted on the 6th February. "It looks like a little town." The tents were used as stores and kennels. Amundsen had no intention of unnecessarily exposing his dogs to the elements.

Now that Bjaaland and Stubberud had finished work on the hut, they started learning to drive dogs. They had plenty of practice, for much still remained to be carried up from the ship. On the 31st January, for example, Amundsen wrote:

> We have moved coal, fur clothes, sledges, and stockfish. It has gone extremely well, even although the going has not been good, after all the snow that has drifted over our route. Every day, we are becoming more organized.

Seal carcasses, however, formed most of Bjaaland and Stubberud's loads. Sometimes as many as twenty seals were shot and flensed in a day so that, as Amundsen put it, "we need not fear a shortage of fresh meat."

Another view of Framheim, early February 1911; snow has begun to drift up on the weather wall. Inside, the last touches were being added. The floor had been covered with linoleum; the walls and loft insulated with cork.

Lt Victor Campbell, Lt H. Pennell, and Dr Murray Levick, of Scott's expedition, had breakfast here when *Terra Nova* put in.

> We had a strange experience [Amundsen wrote afterwards]. We have all caught cold after contact with the Englishmen. We are all sniffing and sneezing.

The cold soon passed over; but the aftertaste of the visit remained. Amundsen had been vividly reminded of his rival or, as he might have felt, the intruder at McMurdo Sound. More than ever, he wanted to start the serious work of preparing for next summer and the polar journey:

> Now there is so little to fetch on board, that there is only work for a few sledges a day. I have therefore decided to go south with 3 men – Johansen, Prestrud and Helmer Hanssen to put out depots. The other 4 will stay here at the base and continue working.

Amundsen was to leave before *Fram* sailed, so he finished his mail and, on the 9th February, went down to say farewell.

Meanwhile, seals somehow made their way over the ice to Framheim, only to be added to the meat store. Amundsen felt he could not have too much in reserve: "An emperor penguin came on a visit – Stockpot."

Scarcely two months later: Framheim at the end of March, 1911, buried up to the eaves in snow. In Amundsen's own words:

> It is quite strange to come out here at night and see the cheerful warm lamplight through the windows of the little snowed-in hut and know [that] our cosy home is on the feared and terrible Barrier.

This was one of many veiled references to Scott who, in his writings, had clothed the Antarctic in an air of romantic mystery. Amundsen, of course, could be romantic himself, but he always swooped back to earth:

Our clever builders have made an extremely practical arrangement. A passage 5 ft. wide has been dug all round the hut [and] roofed in. The covering consists of an extension of the hut roof down to the snow. In this way we have a delightful, closed . . . passage round the whole house. Besides its protective function, it will be of great use as a store for all kinds of things . . . The snow [in] the outer wall [will be] used for drinking water. We simply cut a rectangular hole [and work] through it in the course of the winter. Two things are achieved thereby. I. Always having reliably clean water available – and that is particularly difficult here, with so many puppies loose and mucking up the place. II. Not to be compelled to go into the open to fetch snow. If we have a lot of bad weather, this will be of considerable importance.

Lindstrøm, the cook, leaving *Fram* on the 30th January 1911, to take up his duties at Framheim. He invented a way of serving skua,

> the big bird of carrion [as Amundsen put it], found here in large numbers . . . Cooked like partridge – as Lindstrøm does – it is a most wonderful dish.

Amundsen was a gourmet, but in a hostile environment, food was a matter of survival. Lindstrøm, for example, served seal meat underdone and, in such a way that, with hindsight, vitamin C was obviously conserved. Scurvy was therefore banished from the start.

For breakfast at Framheim – eight o'clock sharp – Lindstrøm served freshly made "hot cakes"; a kind of waffle he had learned to make in Alaska, together with bread and butter, cheese and coffee [Amundsen recorded in his diary]. For dinner, we mostly have seal meat, varied occasionally with tinned food (which we don't really like) . . . For supper: seal steak with whortleberry sauce; bread, butter, cheese and coffee. Every Saturday night, a hot toddy and a cigar. I must openly admit I have never enjoyed myself so much.

Lindstrøm's qualities were not confined to the kitchen. He "made the hut warm and cosy", as Amundsen put it.

He has got the ventilation going; an absolute necessity in an airtight, insulated house like this. Now, it is always dry and airy . . . He has painted the ceiling white, and tidied up everywhere. In the attic, where there was chaos, all boxes have been arranged in numerical order, like soldiers on parade.

Seals being flensed near *Fram*, Bay of Whales, February 1911. So far, the seals in the Ross Sea only knew the enemy in the water: the killer whale cruising among the floes. Man, the predator, was outside their experience. They were therefore easy prey. Amundsen wrote:

> How one becomes hard and unfeeling under such circumstances! By nature I am fond of all animals, and therefore prefer to avoid injuring them. Therefore, it is not at all in my nature to go hunting. It would never occur to me to kill an animal – with the exception of rats and flies – except to sustain life.

On the sea ice, at the Bay of Whales. In the background lies the edge of the Ross Ice Shelf, the Barrier, as Amundsen knew it. The name came from its discoverer, Captain Sir James Clark Ross. He first saw it on 15th January 1841; seventy years before Amundsen landed. Ross's record of the event reads:

> As we approached the land under all studding sails, we perceived a low white line extending . . . as far as the eye could discern eastward. It presented an extraordinary experience, gradually increasing in height as we got nearer to it, and proving at length to be a perpendicular cliff of ice, between one hundred and fifty and two hundred feet above the level of the sea . . . we might with equal chance of success try to sail through the Cliffs of Dover, as to penetrate . . . the icy barrier.

By the time Amundsen arrived, the Barrier was known to be a huge sheet of ice, with a front of about 500 miles, but it was largely unexplored. In Amundsen's projected line of march, it was completely unknown. The question of the day was whether the Barrier was afloat or aground. Amundsen's whole strategy depended on the answer – as far as it could be determined.

Another view of the edge of the Barrier near *Fram*'s landfall at the Bay of Whales. The figure at the top gives an idea of the scale. The snow cover can be seen in the strata on the right. During the past decade, the Barrier had calved, to send icebergs out to sea. The process was bound to repeat itself, none could say exactly when. In making his base here, Amundsen was taking a calculated risk. Observing ridges and folds on the surface of the Barrier he wrote in his diary:

> The irregularities turned out to consist of huge ice blocks on edge. Something must have stopped the barrier in its regular progress and caused this. What else can it be but underlying land? I have no doubt that the whole of this strange, big bay, which has been observed by all previous expeditions, in the same place and – except for a few insignificant changes – with the same appearance, is a formation of underlying land. Otherwise, why should this mighty, even-flowing glacier *always* display at this particular place, an exception to the law it otherwise obeys?

In the light of later knowledge, Amundsen was almost correct. The Ross Ice Shelf is grounded, but some way back, on a shoal today called Roosevelt Island. The Bay of Whales, however, is afloat, but slowed in its advance by the obstruction.

Some of the disturbance in the Barrier round the Bay of Whales, which finally persuaded Amundsen that, in his own words, "Land, land and land again forms this bay. Nothing else." This confirmed the opinion he had already formed from his reading, and which was the foundation of his planning.

Here on the same Barrier where Shackleton praised his God that he had not landed [Amundsen wrote in his diary] – here we will have our home. That Ross did not want to come close to this ice giant in his sailing ships – that I understand. But that S. did not come here and take the great chance offered by an extra degree of Southern latitude; that I don't understand . . . Ah well, perhaps I will meet him one day, and will certainly be able to explain that the terrible Barrier is not so terrible after all.

"Every formation I see in this mighty glacier," Amundsen wrote on arrival at the Bay of Whales, "confirms me in my assumption that disturbances in this inner part only occur very rarely, and therefore we have got nothing to fear from them." Two months later, he observed that "no change has taken place in the Barrier's appearance . . . to the smallest detail, it lies as we saw it last."

In fact, the Bay of Whales moves northwards at a rate of about 500 metres a year. The ice, however, is mostly stable, so that local changes are slow. When the front has advanced far enough, it breaks off, and floats out to sea in the form of large, tabular icebergs. This happens about every ten years.

With food and shelter secured, Amundsen considered the next stage in his plans. This was to be a succession of depot journeys along the route to the Pole before winter set in.

This symbolic snapshot shows Helmer Hanssen, dressed in Netsilik fur garments, posing with some of his dogs. With Eskimo lore, learned on the North West Passage, and the gifts of the Eskimo dog (a better name than husky), Amundsen proposed to win the race for that imaginary point at 90° South.

Helmer Hanssen was incontestably the best dog driver on the expedition. He had empathy with animals. It was his pride that he hardly ever had to resort to the whip. All this had been evident on the North West Passage.

After that expedition, Amundsen had kept contact with Helmer Hanssen and, when the time came, asked him to join the new one. Hanssen had now left the sea, and was working in the Norwegian customs service. Amundsen secured his leave of absence, and offered him 150 *kroner* per month. For Norway in 1909, that was generous. But Amundsen wanted professionals, not amateurs.

Helmer Hanssen once remarked that he had been on the verge of refusing to follow Amundsen when he announced his volte face at Madeira. All along, Amundsen had seen Hanssen's dog driving as the key to reaching the Pole, and getting back in comfort. "Adventure," as someone has said, "is a sign of incompetence."

Amundsen loved photographing his dogs. Fix and Lasse (*above left*), were his favourites. He described how one day

> Lasse escaped and got into a fight with two dogs tethered in the vicinity. During the battle, one of his hind paws got caught in the chains. When we found him, his paw was frozen – hard and white as ice. I thawed it out in my hands. He moaned somewhat. The paw swelled up afterwards. He was [soon] so well that I could put him in my team.

The dogs were naturally pampered, because they were clearly the most important members of the expedition. Without them, the men would have to haul their loads themselves. That would be torture, for which no one on this expedition could drum up much enthusiasm. Not even the South Pole was worth man-hauling, at least to Amundsen and his companions.

*Above right*, Mikkel, the Fox, Else, Masmas, gathered round an unnamed companion lying in the snow. Over a hundred different names had to be found for all the dogs. There was a Major and a Colonel. Hjalmar Johansen called two of his dogs the Scalp and Pimp.

> I have come to the conclusion [he observed] that in dealing with sledge dogs, one will benefit most [if] one assumes that they are at least as intelligent as oneself.

To start with, the dogs were maddeningly rebellious. Amundsen soon discovered why:

> The Alaska style of harnessing, which we use, is quite unusable for these animals, which have been trained with Greenland harnesses.

The Alaskan harness has the dogs attached pair by pair to a central trace. The Greenland fashion has them spreading fanwise from a central point of attachment. Amundsen's experience on the North West Passage persuaded him to adopt the Alaskan system, since it was theoretically more efficient. The dogs, however, were doing the work, so he took the view that they were entitled to their preference:

> I decided to go on board and have [Greenland harnesses] quickly made. Johansen, Hassel and Wisting came with me. With the help of the ship's party, we were able to make 46 sets in the course of an afternoon, or full equipment for the 4 teams we can use at the moment . . . At the same time, we made new traces and connecting links of wire – a long and difficult job.

Amundsen noted the result:

> Things went well with the new harnesses . . . the dogs . . . are now all pulling brilliantly.

Lussi (left), Karenius and The Sheep. Lussi chose the beginning of the polar journey to come into season, of which The Sheep took immediate advantage. "She . . . caused such disorder in the team," Amundsen noted in his diary, "that I found execution the only way of dealing with the matter."

But in February 1911, when this picture was taken that was far in the future. Including pups, Amundsen now had 110 dogs; an increase of 13 since leaving Norway. At Framheim, in his own words, he pitched eight sixteen-man tents as kennels. In order to prevent the dogs attacking the canvas, we have dug down about 4 ft. into the snow. In that way, they will not be able to come in contact with the tent walls. A 16 man tent, in which the floor has been dug down 4 ft., has a huge height, and has the great advantage of a plentiful air supply . . . In the meat tent we have 80 seals cut up for dog food – and out in the snow there are 50 more. Thus we have enough fresh food for our dogs for the winter, even if we have no time to hunt more seals.

Olav Bjaaland at Framheim in the outfit provided for work around the base. By his own account, he joined the expedition "to see the world". Amundsen took him because he was a champion skier.

Bjaaland was 38 when this picture was taken. He came from Telemark, the cradle of modern skiing. In 1902, he had won the Nordic combination, ski jumping and cross-country, at Holmenkollen, the annual Norwegian fixture and, to this day, the classic international Nordic skiing event. In 1908, at the age of 35, he was second in the 50 kilometre race.

The Norwegians pioneered modern skiing, and at the time were still the acknowledged masters. Obviously, the better skiers would win the race for the Pole. For Amundsen, it was an added comfort to have what amounted to a world champion by his side.

When Bjaaland first saw the Barrier from the deck of *Fram*, he wrote:

> It is a strange feeling that grips one as the sight now reveals itself, The sea is still as a pond, and before one stands this Great Wall of China and glitters. Far off, it is like a photograph that has just been developed on the plate.
>
> By letting one's thoughts wander over the surface, one finds oneself in a melancholy mood. One thinks of what is to come, the hardships one is going to meet, the use one will be, and if we can get there before the Englishmen – who are surely burning with the same ambition.

Amundsen's testimonial for Knut Sundbeck, *Fram*'s chief engineer (*above*) reads:

> As engineer and mechanic he is a genius, as a worker conscientious and indefatigable; as a human being, a shining example in all respects.

One of the engineers who had built *Fram*'s motor, Sundbeck was a Swede. Given the old antagonism between Norway and Sweden, he was a brave man to embark with a shipload of Norwegians.

Sundbeck worked for the Atlas Diesel Company, in Stockholm, where the reversible marine diesel was developed. It had only recently gone into production and,

on *Fram*, Sundbeck had the privilege of supervising the first long oceanic voyage ever made under diesel power.

Under sail alone in a storm *Fram* was once taken aback. Sundbeck started the motor, probably saving the ship. His hobby was the search for perpetual motion.

Hjalmar Frederik Gjertsen (*right*) was *Fram*'s second mate. A naval lieutenant in his mid twenties, his explanation for joining the expedition was that "as a schoolboy . . . the ancient Vikings, and, later the great explorers, were my heroes." He desperately wanted to join the shore party, but had to help officer the ship.

On the 10th February Amundsen, together with Prestrud, Johansen, and Helmer Hanssen, left Framheim on their first journey South to depot supplies on the road to the Pole. No one had been that way before; they were breaking a trail into the unknown. On the 14th February, they reached 80°S, and established the first depot (left).

The picture illustrates Amundsen's equipment. The bicycle wheel is part of a sledgemeter, used to log the distance covered. The pile of packing cases in the background, surmounted by a flag, is the depot.

This journey was the first test of Amundsen's preparations. His diary succinctly registers the outcome:

> 11th February. The dogs are pulling magnificently, and the going on the barrier is ideal. Cannot understand what the English mean when they say that dogs cannot be used here.

> 13th February. Today we have had a lot of loose snow . . . for us on skis it was the most magnificent going. How men [on foot] & horses are going to get through in these conditions I cannot understand, not to mention an automobile.

These were references to Scott's transport, and his disparagement of dogs. Arriving back at Framheim on the 15th February, Amundsen returned to the subject:

> A fine performance of our dogs this: 40 geographical miles yesterday – of which 10 miles with heavy load and then 51½ miles today – I think they will hold their own with the ponies on the Barrier.

The route to the depot had been marked with a flag every seven miles and, in Amundsen's own words "every ¼ mile with stockfish and pieces of wood stuck vertically in the snow".

In his diary, Johansen decided that "The so-called Barrier runs like any other glacier." Helmer Hanssen said that "it was much easier to travel down here than up North during the *Gjøa* expedition." The journey had nonetheless revealed various failings, which Amundsen meticulously catalogued:

> Although we got up at 4.15 a.m., we were not ready to start before 7.45 a.m. . . . after 21.5 miles [the] dogs started to be tired . . . our boots proved to be too stiff in the cold . . .

There were two more depot journeys before winter set in. Depots containing a total of three tons of supplies had been advanced to 82°S. That was 140 miles from Framheim, and almost a quarter of the way to the Pole itself. Did he but know it, Amundsen had moved three times as much, 150 miles further than Scott on *his* depot journey, 400 miles to the west.

On his second journey, Amundsen had driven five of his dogs to death.

> It is my only dark memory from down there [he wrote] – that my lovely animals were destroyed. I demanded more of them than they could manage. My consolation is that I did not spare myself either . . .

After his first depot journey, Amundsen returned to Framheim in the evening of the 15th February. "*Fram* had sailed the same morning," he noted in his diary.

> It made a sad, empty impression on all of us. But I hope the time will come when we meet again with work well done.

This picture shows *Fram* leaving the Bay of Whales, to spend the winter outside the polar regions, and avoid being frozen in. Before heading out to sea, she swung into the innermost part of the Bay of Whales, to reach 78°41′S, and keep her record of being the ship to have been both furthest north and furthest south.

*Fram* was bound for Buenos Aires, where she arrived two months later. Nilsen had been led to believe that money would have been sent there from Norway. None had arrived, for the simple reason that Amundsen had left nothing but debts behind, and the expedition was insolvent. Don Pedro Christopherson, Amundsen's last-minute benefactor, came to the rescue, paying all the expenses of Amundsen's relief.

Meanwhile, on the 8th June, *Fram* sailed, as planned, on an oceanographic cruise between South America and southern Africa. She returned to Buenos Aires on the 1st September.

Expedition members on the sea ice at the Bay of Whales. Alexander Kutchin (left), oceanographer; Thorvald Nilsen, *Fram*'s captain; Martin Rønne, sailmaker; Ludvig Hansen, ice pilot; Halvardus Kristensen, third engineer; Lindstrøm; Fr. Hj. Gjertsen, first mate; Knut Sundbeck, chief engineer; Karenius Olsen, ship's cook; and Jakob Nødtvedt, second engineer.

All except Lindstrøm belonged to the ship's party. Kutchin was a Russian studying in Norway. He was a pupil of Bjørn Helland-Hansen, one of the founders of modern oceanography, and also one of the few to whom Amundsen had revealed in advance that he was going south. Kutchin was on board at Helland-Hansen's request. "His wages," as Amundsen had put it, "will be 60 kroner per month and good treatment."

On the 19th April 1911, the sun disappeared at Framheim for the winter, not to reappear for four months. Next day, in Amundsen's words,

> we began to extend our premises. Along the axis of the house, facing west, a huge snowdrift had formed just in front of the entrance. It was our intention . . . to remove it. At the last moment, it occurred to me that we could possibly use the drift and escape the work of shovelling and carting it away. We have now started to excavate it and arrange a direct connection with the house through an underground passage. By digging downwards, we can obtain all the space we need. Provisionally, we are digging out a carpenter's workshop for Bjaaland and Stubberud . . . I think the idea is good!

Above, one of the passages, with steps, under the snow.

The winter was long, but hardly long enough to prepare for the polar journey; especially remedying all the defects in equipment revealed so far. On the right, the wintering party are modelling their personalized snow goggles. Hassel (left), Bjaaland, Wisting, Helmer Hanssen, Amundsen, Johansen, (standing) Lindstrøm, Prestrud and Stubberud. They are sitting round the table in the hut at midwinter.

> Our excavation of . . . workshops . . . under the snow [said Amundsen], has repaid itself many times. How would it look in our only living space if we had dragged in sledges, ski, tents . . . etc. . . . discontent all along the line . . . Everybody always in each others' way.

Sverre Hassel in his vault underneath the snow, during the southern winter of 1911. Hassel, as Amundsen whimsically wrote in his diary, was

> director of the "Framheim Coal, Wood and Petroleum Co." – an extremely responsible position. He is everything rolled into one: from director – or possibly, chairman of the board – to messenger boy.

The drums in the picture contain two grades of paraffin, to be used according to temperature. It was used for lighting; also for heating the workshops under the snow. Around midwinter, Amundsen recorded "−51.8° outside . . . In the snow workshops it has been very warm . . . +3 to 4°."

The paraffin was also the vital fuel for the Primus stoves used for cooking on the march. Already 100 litres were waiting in the depots as far as 82°S. Amundsen was working with huge margins of safety; probably 300 per cent or more.

Hassel also had a workshop under the snow where he was

> preparing thongs for dog whips [as Amundsen put it]. These instruments of torture for our wonderful animals are now produced every day. It is a great pity that this is necessary; but there is no way out. Making these thongs is not quick work. The thongs are of sealskin, softened in train oil, and worked so that they attain the greatest possible weight and flexibility – both essential if one is to hit the dog for which one is aiming with any certainty. In addition [Hassel] has to keep the hut supplied with coal [for cooking].

Prestrud (left) and Helmer Hanssen lashing provision cases on the sledges to be used on the polar journey. Their workshop also lay underneath the snow.

The cases were made of solid ash, but, in Amundsen's words, the wood

> was too thick, and we have had a lot of work to make it thinner. The plane would not cut, so [the wood] first had to be shaved off with an axe. The work has been done by Stubberud, with the assistance of Prestrud. [The wood] is now only 5 mm. thick. Good material is necessary, if the [cases] are to bear the 80 kilos which some will have to do. Aluminium reinforcements had been fitted to the corners . . . All cases have small aluminium lids, which can be removed without touching the lashings. The lashings are fixed, and consist of 4 thin wires permanently attached to the sledges.

The cases were to be permanently attached to the sledges throughout the polar journey. This was to save time and energy and thus, in Amundsen's opinion, increase the margin of safety.

It was conceivable, Amundsen noted in his diary, that

> one might be affected by the [winter] darkness. But no – we are cheerful . . . We are always busy, and that is the main thing in wintering.

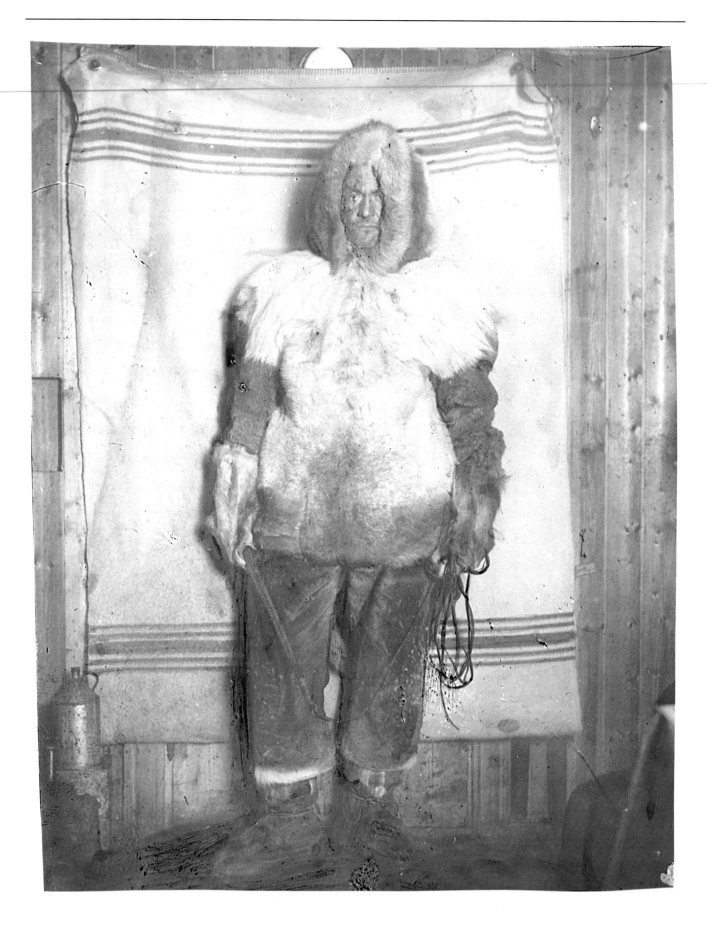

*Above*] Part of the kitchen at Framheim. Here, Lind-ström made his "hot cakes", the breakfast dish which became the gastronomic memory of the expedition. Here too, he carried out his instrument repairs. As Amundsen put it,

> besides his kitchen duties, he is called upon when mechanical ingenuity is required . . . Lindström constantly surprises me. I thought I knew him well, but he constantly reveals unknown sides of himself . . . Our sledgemeters were badly made . . . He now has got them in order. [He repaired] an unusable thermograph . . . He has made our photographic safelight . . . usable.

The device high up to the right is the thermograph (recording thermometer) under test. The two cylindrical objects on the wall are mercury barometers.

In the kitchen, too, Prestrud gave English lessons to Wisting, Helmer Hanssen, Stubberud and Bjaaland, so that they could read Shackleton's and Scott's books in Framheim's polar library. Prestrud also gave a course in navigation which everyone, including Amundsen, attended.

*Left*] Kristian Prestrud, at Framheim during the winter, posing in cold weather fur outfit, holding dog whip.

Hjalmar Johansen packing provisions for the polar journey. "Everything is advancing slowly, but with great care and precision," Amundsen wrote on the 9th June 1911.

I hope that we can find place for all provisions in 4 cases per sledge = 28 cases in all. The packing must therefore be carried out with the greatest care. Not a millimetre must be wasted. And Johansen is the man – extremely careful and conscientious.

To save weight, the pemmican – packed in half kilo portions – was removed from the tins but, Amundsen noted, its shape.

was cylindrical. This is . . . unfortunate . . . because [when packed they] leave a space . . . difficult to fill. Well, difficulties have not yet frightened us . . . These spaces, which are 4 cm.

across and as high as the case – 39 cm. – are filled with milk powder. On his sewing machine, Wisting has sewn the necessary 189 sausage skins of thin material, and I have filled them with milk powder . . . each sausage holds 300 gm, which is exactly what a tent team – 4 men – needs for their hot chocolate. Thus it is easy to obtain one's dried milk by extracting a sausage.

In the picture, Johansen is showing these "sausages" arranged in one of the boxes.

Packing of the biscuit boxes, said Amundsen,

is the *greatest* test of patience, because [Johansen] has to stow 5 to 6,000 sledging biscuits precisely side by side . . . so as not to waste any space. And [he] has managed it particularly well.

Another workshop under the snow. On the 5th July 1911, Amundsen wrote:

> Wisting is sitting *in* the Great Ice Barrier and sewing tents on his Singer – in +14°. To stop water dripping, he has lined his snowy sewing room with blankets . . . and these insulate extraordinarily well. The sewing machine is a little sleepy first thing in the morning, but later on works well . . . He is sewing new, light groundsheets in [the tents]. By this means, we save several kilos.

This was the second time Wisting had to modify the sledging tents. Originally, they had been made for two men, but this soon proved unsatisfactory. After the first depot journey, they were sewn together in pairs, to hold four or five men each.

Amundsen had also been dissatisfied with the original colour:

> Our sledging tents are of thin, white cloth, and that will be no good in the spring, when the sun is high. It will then be far preferable to have a dark tent, into which one can go after the day's work, and rest one's eyes. Another consideration is that a dark colour will absorb the sun's rays to a greater degree, and make the tent warm. Ah well, we rarely allow ourselves to be defeated. We have made a mixture of ink powder, and black boot polish, and with that product, we will get our tents as dark as we want.

Olav Bjaaland planing down sledge runners in his underground workshop. Amundsen had been misled by Shackleton and Scott into believing that the terrain was rougher than it turned out to be. In fact the Barrier, with its gently rolling expanses, and firm snow crust, was well nigh ideal for skiers. In Amundsen's words:

> It was apparent that the old sledges could be considerably reduced in weight . . . The loose runners are being planed down by half.

A month later, on the 22nd June, he wrote that

> Today, Bjaaland finished the first new sledge. It is extremely fine to look at, and is particularly light – 24 kilos – against 34 kilos [previously].

By the 14th July, Bjaaland had finished all the sledges, and then started preparing the ski.

> Everyone [Amundsen explained] will have two pairs of ski. On the first pair, intended for daily use during the polar journey – fixed bindings [in one piece] will be used – the original Huitfeldt bindings. On the other – to be taken [on a sledge] as a spare pair – Bjaaland is making binding ears in two parts, so that they can be mounted during the journey, if necessary. The point is, it will take too much space to have the bindings attached.

Amundsen's boot and bindings, in their final form. The binding is of the Huitfeldt-Høier-Ellefsen pattern; the first satisfactory heel binding. The heel clip was the first quick release device on the market.

The boots were specially made for the expedition; the bindings bought commercially. Both had to be altered, as Amundsen explained:

These boots, which were as capacious as any shoemaker in Kristiania would agree to, nonetheless proved to be too small . . . They were made of thin leather and canvas. On the first depot journey, the boots already proved not to fulfil our requirements – soft and roomy. In the first place, the canvas was removed & replaced with soft windproof cloth. In that form, I used them on the second depot journey . . . and was extremely satisfied. But then they proved [to be] too tight around the toes, and had to be altered. Wisting, like the craftsman he is . . . has done this for me . . . brilliantly . . . A big wedge has been inserted in the toe cap . . . I can now put it on with the greatest ease, when I am wearing reindeer socks, with plenty of sennegrass, thick rag socks & heavy winter kamikk and still move my foot freely inside.

The bindings, Amundsen wrote, with their leather heel straps,

had to be protected against the dogs. We know that within a few days they will consider our bindings the greatest delicacy. [They have been improved] so that we can easily detach them in the evenings and take them into the tent. That will fox the hounds!

The entrance to the hut at Framheim during the winter; a photograph taken by moonlight. A black and white film without colour correction, together with some retouching, gives an unfamiliar effect. Amundsen described the scene in his diary for the 22nd May, 1911:

Good weather. Still and clear −46° . . . Tomorrow we will have the door to the entrance installed, and thereby the whole of this huge snow complex will be finished . . . It is difficult to describe the beautiful scene I saw when I came out of my dog tent this afternoon. Low down on the S.W. horizon was the moon – shining yellow – just over the rooftop of our hut – or snow mound. In the S.W. sky the Southern Lights played in many forms and colours – and high up there one sees the Southern Cross among an army of glittering, shining worlds. Like a fairy tale, the big, pointed . . . tents rise up, all illuminated as if in celebration . . . If only I could paint – if only I could.

"We are all happy," Amundsen wrote about this time. "Our dogs likewise. They are constantly putting on weight, and are now as fat as pigs."

These are happy days. Please God, may they continue, and carry us through to the goal we all long to reach.

23rd August 1911. Amundsen wrote in his diary: "The polar journey has begun." The sledges, ready loaded, were hauled by block and tackle out of the workshops under the snow. Next day, the sun returned. On the 8th September, Amundsen, with seven companions, set off for the south, leaving Lindstrøm to look after Framheim alone.

It was a false start. A week later, Amundsen was back again, defeated by the cold. He recorded temperatures down to −55.5°. A bottle of Geneva was frozen solid; so too was the liquid in the compasses. Men were frostbitten; five dogs froze to death. On the 20th September, Amundsen wrote that he had

made what I hope is the final decision on our future work. We will be divided into two parties. To the south go Helmer Hanssen, Wisting, Hassel, Bjaaland and I. Prestrud, [Johansen] and Stubberud go east to determine the position of King Edward VII Land . . . Our departure is set for the 15th October at the earliest. My intention is to wait longer if weather and circumstances require it. We must go forwards – but care is needed.

Scott was preying on his mind. Of his and Shackleton's earlier expeditions, Amundsen had written that

Either the Englishmen must have had bad dogs or – they didn't know how to use them . . . The English have loudly and openly told the world that skis and dogs are unusable in these regions and that fur clothes are rubbish. We will see – we will see.

Lindstrøm, wind gauge in hand, photographed next to the meteorological screen that he made at Framheim.

> He is very proud of it [said Amundsen], and he had every reason to be. It is perfect in every detail – a first-class carpenter could not have done it better . . . Trusting . . . cheerful and willing, a better man has never set foot inside the polar regions. I hope from the bottom of my heart to be in a position one day to do something for him. He has done Norwegian polar exploration greater service than anyone else.

Not even Lindstrøm was able to cheer up the inhabitants of Framheim, as they waited for the polar journey to begin. The false start, and subsequent quarrel between Amundsen and Johansen, had left an unhappy atmosphere.

The day after returning to Framheim, Amundsen recorded the incident in his diary:

> At the breakfast table . . . Johansen found it suitable to utter unflattering statements about me and my position as leader for our enterprise here. It was not only our return yesterday that he found indefensible in the highest degree, *but* also much else I had taken the liberty of doing as leader in the course of time. The gross and unforgivable part of [Johansen's statements] is that they were made in everybody's hearing. The bull must be taken by the horns; I must make an example immediately.

This was the reason that Johansen was now going to King Edward VII Land, and not to the Pole.

Friday, 20th October 1911; sledges ready for the start of the polar journey. Amundsen's diary reads:

At last, we got away. The weather was not quite reliable . . . 9.30 a.m., it cleared in the east, with light breeze. We saddled our steeds; 13 before each of the 4 sledges, and set off. Prestrud stood with the kinomatograph during the descent to the sea ice and got us all. A few seals lay about, including a few newborn pups. He shot us again during our climb on the other side of the bay. The weather came down after we had gone a little way over the Barrier. HH [Helmer Hanssen] was running first and steered by compass. Somehow we strayed too far to the east, and into unknown terrain full of crevasses. I sat with Wisting. His sledge was the last. Suddenly a large piece of the surface disappeared, and a gaping abyss opened next to the sledge – big enough to swallow us all. Luckily we were off to one side, so we managed.

Amundsen had no sledge of his own. On the abortive start, they had dumped their loads at the 80° depot, so were running relatively light.

We changed course directly east by compass (S.W. true). That soon brought us within sight of a flag [marking the route] and soon after we reached the place where we shot "Kaisa" – day's run 20.2 miles. We were extremely comfortable in our improved tent. We are 5, but have plenty of room.

On the 23rd October, Amundsen reached his depot at 80°S. He found it in thick drift, "unable to see our hands in front of our faces," as he said.

It was a brilliant test. A single point on this vast plain found with sledgemeter and compass.

They stayed there two days; amongst other things to dig the depot out, rebuild it, and check the position once more with an observation of the sun. This is what the photograph illustrates.

This depot contained a ton of seal meat and, as Amundsen wrote in his diary,

We have given the dogs plenty of seal meat and [seal] carcasses lie out on the snow for unlimited use . . . We now have 4 dogs fewer than when we set off. These 4 were let loose along the way, as they could not keep up, presumably from overeating. Therefore we now have 48 dogs, or 4 teams of 12 each. We are enjoying ourselves in the tent. We had the good idea of making an outer tent out of our red bunk curtains [at Framheim]. This . . . has been excellent, since it has reduced the warmth of the sun . . . while holding the warmth inside. It is an amazing difference from the previous journey. Now we lie in loose sleeping clothes – nice and warm. Another great advantage is that the tent is dark inside. [It was light now round the clock] and that is desirable, when one has been staring at the snow all day . . . The dogs are enjoying life.

Amundsen noted that he brought to the depot at 80°S:

200 kilos dog pemmican + 30 litres paraffin + 2 tins of meat + 3 alpine ropes + 3 complete rations for 100 days. We have taken from the depot: 1 case of paraffin + 5 seals [for the dogs to eat there] + 15 kilos seal fillets + 8 packets of chocolate.

The picture shows Bjaaland preparing to solder a paraffin tank at the depot so that it was hermetically sealed, and none of the contents could escape. One of these tanks was found fifty years later in the snow, with its contents still intact. The empty sledge seen here lying on its side was a spare one, dumped for an emergency.

On the 26th October, Amundsen left the depot first, however, tidying up:

We gathered all seal meat in one place . . . collected all pieces of blubber strewn over the snow, and put finishing touches to the depot. We started at 9 a.m. The dogs were absolutely wild. We did our distance, 15 nautical miles, by 12 noon. Made camp. Wonderful weather. The Barrier was completely even over this stretch. The going was splendid.

*Left*] 30th October 1911; arriving at the depot at 81°S. "The weather was not of the best kind," as Amundsen put it. Nor was the snow:

> small sastrugi [wind-blown ridges in the snow] loose drift . . . at 1 p.m. the depot hove into view. Our course was almost dead on. Arrived 2 p.m. Everything in order. Judging by appearances, very little snow has fallen. The snowdrift round the depot is about 1½ ft. high. Our average speed is now 3 nautical miles an hour.

Next day was a rest day. "Bjaaland and I," Amundsen noted in his diary,

> went out to examine the transverse marking. These marks were narrow packing case boards about 2½ ft. long and were put out at the beginning of March [this year]. There they were now, at the end of October, just as they had been. They were about ½ft. lower – presumably affected by drift. They were so clear, that we could not possibly have passed without seeing them.

This was a device to find the depot in any weather. Amundsen had been deeply impressed by the horrific tales told by Scott and Shackleton of nearly missing depots because of inadequate marking. In the middle of the great snow plain, there were no landmarks, and Amundsen did not propose to repeat past mistakes.

*Above*] This slide was prepared by Amundsen for explaining this system of transverse marking to his English-speaking audiences. On either side of the depot were ten flags at one mile intervals, each numbered as indicated. This meant that in the thickest weather, a single flag was enough to point the way. Since the flags stretched ten miles on either side, the chances of missing one were remote. The conical shapes placed along the line of march are snow cairns seven miles apart, also numbered, to help in finding the depot.

Amundsen stopped regularly to build a snow cairn, in order to mark the route and guide him back. This picture shows such a stop on the Barrier, with cairn completed. The cairns were three miles apart, or about forty-five minutes' travel. This distance was chosen because dogs like frequent rests and, in clear weather, one cairn would be visible from the other.

On the 1st November, the day after leaving the 81° depot, Amundsen ran into thick fog and, despite all precautions, strayed off the track too far to the east.

> We found crevasse after crevasse [he wrote]. They were not particularly wide – about 3 ft. – and luckily ran across our course . . . When we had done 12.5 nautical miles, Helmer Hanssen – who always goes first – drove over a crevasse, and was so unlucky as to catch his ski tip in one of the traces while he was right over the crevasse, and fell across the crevasse. A fairly unpleasant situation. The dogs had reached the other side, and started a horrible battle on the edge of the abyss. Meanwhile, the sledge remained half sunk in the crevasse, and threatened to fall in at any time. I was able to stop the dog fight. Wisting dragged Helmer Hanssen away from his perilous position, and with our united strength, we were able to drag the sledge away from the dangerous neighbourhood.

The following day, they had escaped from the crevassed terrain, but the weather remained bad. Amundsen's diary for the 4th November reads:

> We stopped after having done 16 nautical miles. We have thus done the distance to 82°. We see no sign of the depot, but that is only to be expected, since the weather has well and truly come down.

Next day:

> At 4 a.m. the sun came out for a moment and we were not slow in getting out of our sleeping bags. There the depot loomed up about 2 miles ESE. The small flags were just as they had been left, standing out beautifully against the white background. This is a victory for us. We have shown that it is possible to lay out depots in these endless expanses and mark them so that with careful navigation we can find them again. We took the depot's bearings, and got back into bed again. After breakfast we packed up and set off. It had then closed in again, but we had our bearing, and after 2½ miles' march we stood by our southernmost depot. Everything was in the finest order.

This was the furthest depot put out the previous autumn. On the 7th November, when Amundsen left 82°, after a day's rest, his sledges were fully loaded, but now he was truly on his own.

On the Barrier Amundsen continued laying depots every degree of latitude. That enabled him to shed weight, while securing his retreat. He used this picture to illustrate the depot both at 81°S and 84°S. It is probably the latter.

He reached the depot on the 13th November 1911. By then, he had discovered an unknown mountain range in the distance straddling his path. He called it the Queen Maud Range, after the Queen of Norway. His diary reads:

> Glittering white, shining blue, raven black, in the light of the sun, the land looks like a fairy tale. Pinnacle after pinnacle, peak after peak – crevassed, wild as any land on our globe, it lies, unseen and untrodden. It is a wonderful feeling to travel along it.

Amundsen had to find a way across. His timetable allowed him a week. Shackleton, who had pioneered Scott's route through the continuation of these mountains over to the west, had taken a fortnight.

> We are naturally very excited [Amundsen wrote]. Tomorrow should have been a rest day, but we all agree we must profit by the good weather. The dogs do not give the impression of being exhausted.

On the 18th November, Amundsen began the mountain crossing.

Amundsen's photograph of Mount Don Pedro Christoph-erson, named after his great benefactor. It overlooks the Axel Heiberg Glacier, named after another of Amundsen's patrons, and his route across the mountains to the polar plateau. Amundsen first compared it with a fjord, but later wrote:

We . . . stopped to find a way out of the giant, chaotic crevasses that surround us. Huge ice blocks, mighty abysses and huge crevasses block our path . . . It seemed rather difficult to find a way ahead, but after a 5 hour reconnaissance Helmer Hanssen and Bjaaland succeeded in finding a reasonably usable pass . . . we found good [snow] bridges everywhere. The glacier . . . was fairly steep in a number of places, and relaying with double teams had to be resorted to.

On the 21st November, Amundsen wrote:

So we won through. We are lying on the plateau at 10,600 ft. altitude. It has been a hard day – mostly for the dogs. But 24 of our brave companions received the bitter wage – death. On arrival they were shot.

This was to save food. After the climb, they were no longer needed.

The 18 best remain . . . It was a marvel what the dogs did today. 17 nautical miles and 5,000 [ft.] climb. Come and say that dogs cannot be used here. In 4 days, we have climbed from the coast to the plateau – 44 nautical miles – 10,600 ft.

The Devil's Glacier, near the head of the Axel Heiberg Glacier. On the 30th November 1911, Amundsen wrote:

> The Devil's Glacier was worthy of its name. One has to move 2 miles to advance 1. Chasm after chasm, abyss after abyss has to be circumvented. Treacherous crevasses and much other unpleasantness make progress extremely hard. The dogs are struggling, and the drivers not less.

This picture shows the party after crossing the snow bridge in the foreground. Someone has gone across sideways on ski to test the snow and prepare the surface for dogs and sledges. Next day, Amundsen wrote:

How often have I not discovered that a day one expects nothing of – brings much. A south easterly blizzard . . . overnight had half persuaded me to declare a rest day for the dogs. But, during a little lull, we agreed to try and travel. It was cold to begin with. During the night the wind had swept large areas of the glacier bare and free of snow. The crevasses were horrible . . . But we managed inch by inch, foot by foot, sledge length by sledge length, sometimes east, sometimes west, sometimes north, sometimes south, round huge open chasms and treacherous crevasses about to collapse . . . But we managed and, after a time [moving in] fog, gale and drift [we found] the chasms more and more filled with snow . . . until we reached the plateau, where they completely ceased.

Amundsen was not yet out of the wood; after the Devil's Glacier, he still had to face the Devil's Ballroom (*above*). He described it in his diary for the 4th December:

> First we had to cross . . . mirror-smooth ice with filled crevasses here and there. This . . . was not difficult to cross . . . Naturally, there was no question of using ski. We all had to support the sledges and help the dogs. The next terrain offered good going, and we congratulated ourselves on having overcome all difficulties. But no! We were not going to get off so lightly. [We encountered] a violent disturbance [in the ice]. Suddenly one of the runners of Wisting's sledge broke through to a bottomless crevasse . . . We were able to hoist it up again without damage . . . We got through safe and sound and climbed up on a rise. This again consisted of bare ice, but then we discovered it to be filled with hidden crevasses, where we could not set our foot anywhere without breaking through.

This is the passage that the picture portrays.

> Luckily most of these crevasses were filled, but some were dangerous enough. It was hard work for the dogs. Bjaaland fell through, but managed to hold on to his sledge, otherwise he would have been irrevocably lost . . . We finally got over, and little by little [the terrain] changed to the real plateau, without any disturbance . . . No more chasms or crevasses –

Amundsen had now reached 87°S. He was 180 miles from the Pole.

From Amundsen's diary for the 8th December 1911:

One of our big days. This morning . . . the weather was thick,
with poor visibility, as usual. But . . . the terrain and skiing
were of the best kind . . . We had not been travelling long,
before it began to clear a little all round the horizon. [At
midday] the sun appeared, not in all its glory, but . . . enough
for a good observation . . . We had not had an observation
since 86°47'S, and it was essential to establish our position
. . . the result was almost exactly 88°16'. A splendid victory
after 1½° march in thick fog and snowdrift. Our observation
and dead reckoning agreed to the minute . . . So now we are
ready to take the Pole in any kind of weather . . . From the
point where we took the observation to the Englishmen's
(Shackleton's) world record only 7 miles remain. (88°23.) I had
given HH [Helmer Hanssen] our Pole flag, which he was to
hoist on his sledge – the leading sledge – as soon as this was
passed. I myself was forerunner at the time. The weather had
improved, and the sun had broken through properly. My snow
goggles bothered me from time to time. A gentle breeze from
the south made them mist over, so that it was difficult to see.
Then I suddenly heard a stout, hearty cheer behind. I turned
round. In the light breeze from the south, the brave, well-
known colours [of the Norwegian flag] waved from the first
sledge, we have passed and put behind us the Englishmen's
record. It was a splendid sight. The sun had just broken
through in all its glory . . . My goggles clouded over again,
but this time it was not the south wind's fault.

This picture recorded the scene.
Next day was a rest day, so that, in Amundsen's words,

We can prepare for the final onslaught. We laid a depot here
to lighten the sledges . . . Bjaaland's dogs have lost so much
weight recently and yesterday one of Wisting's dogs – "The
Major" – a sturdy old dog, disappeared.

During the winter, Amundsen had written of the dogs:

Faithful are they, faithful unto death. It hurts me to think that
our faithful companions, our dear friends, will presumably all
receive death as payment for faithful service – Feelings will
luckily not be so sensitive when we have covered so much of
our journey, that this is on the cards.

This did not quite turn out to be the case. The slaughter
of the dogs at the top of the Axel Heiberg glacier was a
terrible experience. The place was called the Butcher's
Shop. Amundsen was exceedingly glad to put it behind
him.

Nonetheless, the fresh meat, fed to the other dogs,
probably saved their lives and, in consequence those of
their masters too.

"So we arrived, and planted our flag at the geographical South Pole," Amundsen wrote in his diary. "Thanks be to God!"

The entry was headed: "Friday 15 December (really 14th). When *Fram* crossed the International Date Line on her way to Antarctica, Amundsen had forgotten to drop a day. His calendar therefore was one day out; but this date had to be correct.

This picture was taken soon after arrival at the Pole. Oscar Wisting (left), Olav Bjaaland, Sverre Hassel and Amundsen. Helmer Hanssen took this photograph with Bjaaland's camera.

Amundsen's diary continues:

The time was 3 p.m. when it happened. The weather was of the finest sort when we started this morning, but around 10 a.m., it became overcast. Fresh breeze from SE. The going has been partly good, partly bad. The plain – King Haakon VII's Plateau – has had the same appearance – quite flat and without what one can call sastrugi. The sun came out again during the afternoon, and we ought to get a midnight observation . . . We arrived here with 3 sledges and 17 dogs. Helmer Hanssen put one down immediately after arrival. "Helgi" was worn out. Tomorrow we will go out in 3 directions to ring in the polar area. We have eaten our celebratory meal – a little piece of seal meat each.

Helmer Hanssen with his dog team on arrival at the South Pole, 14th December 1911. It was, as he wrote afterwards,

a solemn moment for us all. As always, Amundsen thought of his companions, and when we planted the Norwegian flag at the South Pole, he let us all hold the bamboo stick with the flag, when it was fixed in the snow . . . For my part, I had no feeling of triumph at that moment – as perhaps might have been expected. I was relieved to know that no longer would I have to stare down at the compass in the biting wind, which continually blew against us while we drove southwards, but which we now would have behind us.

Oscar Wisting (*right*), with his dog team on arrival at the South Pole, at 3 p.m. on the 14th December, 1911. Afterwards he recalled that

Roald Amundsen asked us to gather round to plant the flag. "It is not the privilege of one man alone to carry out this

ceremony. It is the privilege of all those," he said, "who have risked their lives for this cause." Each man gripped the flagpole, and together we planted Norway's flag at the South Pole, where no human being had yet set foot.

The following day, as Amundsen put it, was "extremely agitated".

We turned out at midnight to shoot the sun . . . Calculations put us at about 89°56′ [4 miles from the Pole]. That wasn't too bad. At 2.30 a.m., Bjaaland, Wisting and Hassel went off on ski to ring the Pole. Bjaaland continued along our original course NE by N (compass) while Hassel went NW by W (compass) and Wisting SE by E (compass). They were to cover a distance of about 10 nautical miles. They each had a post (spare sledge runner) with a black flag. To each post was attached a little bag containing information on where "Polheimen" ["The home of the Pole"] lay. The weather was glorious. Calm, but a little misty . . . at 10 a.m. they were all back again.

Olav Bjaaland, together with his dogs on arrival at the South Pole, 14th December 1911. He recorded the day in his diary:

> So now we have attained the goal of our desires, and the great thing is that we are here as the first men, no English flag is waving, but a 3 coloured Norwegian. We have now eaten and drunk our fill of what we can manage; seal steak, and biscuits and pemmican and chocolate.
>
> Yes, if only you knew *mother*, and you Susanna and T. and Svein and Helga and Hans, that now I'm sitting here at the South Pole and writing, you'd celebrate for me. Here it's as flat as the lake at Morgedal [Bjaaland's home] and the skiing is good.

Bjaaland, Helmer Hanssen and Wisting were driving sledges on arrival at the Pole, which is why they alone were photographed with dog teams. Amundsen had no dogs from the start because, as leader, he felt he had to be unattached. Hassel lost his team at the Butcher's Shop.

The dogs were now reorganized into two teams, leaving Wisting and Helmer Hanssen as the remaining drivers. Bjaaland's comment was short and to the point: "Thank God I am quit the fuss and bother of my dogs."

"Shooting the sun" at the South Geographical Pole. Amundsen (left) is holding a sextant. Helmer Hanssen (right) is bending over the "artificial horizon", which is a tray of mercury. Amundsen is lining up the direct image of the sun with its reflection in the surface of the mercury. This is a device to circumvent the lack of a true horizon on land.

It is quite interesting to see the sun wander round the heavens at so to speak the same altitude day and night [Amundsen wrote in his diary]. I think somehow we are the first to see this curious sight.

Two days after arriving at the Pole, Amundsen moved his camp five and a half miles to the position of the Pole indicated by preliminary calculations. There, for a whole day and night, he took hourly observations. The dogs, he noted in his diary,

are all lying stretched out in the heat of the sun, enjoying life, in spite of little food. They seem to be quite well. It has been so clear today, that we have been able to see for miles around. We have all used our telescopes industriously to see if there is any sign of life in any direction – but in vain. We are the first here all right.

"And so farewell, dear Pole," Amundsen wrote in his diary, "I don't think we'll meet again." Amundsen (left), Helmer Hanssen, Hassel and Wisting, just before leaving the Pole on the 18th December 1911 – or 17th December true reckoning. Either way, they had spent three days there.

The tent was that made by Rønne on the voyage out (see p. 62), and taken for emergencies. It was now left behind to mark the Pole. In his diary, Amundsen noted that

the Norwegian flag, with the *Fram* pennant underneath, are flying from the top of the tent pole. In the tent, I have placed various things: my sextant with a glass artificial horizon [the party still had another sextant], a hypsometer [instrument for measuring altitude by the boiling point of water], 3 reindeer fur boot warmers, some kamikks [Eskimo fur boots], and mittens, and a few small things. In a folder, I left a letter for the King [of Norway] and some words to Scott who, I must assume, will be the first to visit the place after us.

While Amundsen was in the South, Prestrud, Johansen and Stubberud were on their journey east of Framheim towards King Edward VII Land. This was about 100 miles off, against 680 miles to the South Pole. It was a sideshow, of which they were only too aware. It was the aftermath of the abortive start for the Pole in September.

On that occasion, Prestrud had proved not to be strong enough for the main journey. The quarrel between Amundsen and Johansen precluded their being on the same party. Stubberud had joined them to make up the numbers, at Amundsen's urgent request.

This picture, taken on the journey, shows Stubberud (left) and Johansen sounding through a crack in the sea ice close to the edge of the Ross Ice Shelf, or the Barrier, as they knew it. They improvised a lead out of a geological hammer and sewing thread.

Prestrud, Johansen and Stubberud left Framheim on the 8th November 1911. They reached King Edward VII Land on the 2nd December.

King Edward VII Land had been discovered on the 30th January 1902 during the cruise of the *Discovery*, under Scott. This picture shows Johansen (left) and Stubberud on a rocky outcrop, subsequently named Scott's Nunatak. The flag flying from the improvised flagstaff is to show that the Norwegians were the first actually to set foot on King Edward VII Land (King Edward Peninsula today).

For us, who had stared ourselves silly on a blinding white endlessness of snow and ice for nearly a year [wrote Prestrud], it was a wonderful experience to see a piece of the earth's crust again . . . During the first few moments after "landing", we possibly acted a little childishly. In any case, I observed one, who shall be nameless, who apparently found great satisfaction in pushing one boulder after the other down the nunatak's steep slopes.

Between the 4th and 7th December, Prestrud's party was tentbound in a blizzard on King Edward VII Land. Snow was falling which, in the Antarctic, is a rarity. Antarctica is one of the great deserts of the world, and most storms simply whip snowdrift from one place to another, like sandstorms in the cold.

This photograph shows the scene after the storm. The objects rigged on the ski sticks are reindeer fur sleeping bags – used by the whole expedition – hanging out to dry. The figure on the left is digging out the sledge.

On the 11th January 1912, Prestrud was back at Framheim, to find that *Fram* had arrived two days earlier. On the 16th January, in the words of Thorvald Nilsen, *Fram*'s captain,

> we were a little surprised to see a vessel come in . . . finally we saw the Japanese flag. I had no idea that the expedition was on the way again.

The ship was called *Kainan Maru* ("Opener up of the South"). This picture shows her anchored near Framheim. This was the first Japanese Antarctic expedition.

The year before, *Kainan Maru* had failed to reach Antarctica, and wintered in Australia. Nilsen noted in his diary that her captain,

> Hamura, was on board [*Fram*]. His aim was not (?) the Pole. In all, they had 25 (27?) men on board, 2 Ainus [tribesmen from Sakhalin] to drive their dogs, of which they had 27. They mostly eat vegetables, as far as I understand . . . Together with Prestrud, I went on board *Kainan Maru*. It is a small, extremely dirty vessel of about 200 tons. Everything seems to be very disorganized. A seal lay half dead on the ice; they only stood around and laughed at it. It we had had some firearms with us, we would have put it out of its misery . . . they are really *quite* wild. We spoke "English" with them.

Some of *Kainan Maru*'s crew at the Bay of Whales. The Norwegians were somewhat perturbed, because the Japanese had occupied a tent they had pitched on a headland for a lookout.

On the 26th January 1912, the polar party stood on the Barrier overlooking the Bay of Whales.

> Before we realized it [Amundsen wrote in his diary], we had returned to our point of departure. "Framheim" was as we had left it, bathed in the morning light. It did not take us long to cross the bay, and at 4 a.m., we were once more inside our comfortable little house – welcomed heartily by our . . . companions, who were not expecting us for a long time yet.

This picture shows the entrance to the hut at Framheim, complete with guardian, as it appeared to Amundsen that morning.

The return from the Pole had been no more than a long ski tour. Bjaaland, the old ski champion, summed it up by saying: "It was a damned hard job being forerunner." He had led all the way from the Pole; 700 miles, more or less.

There had been one hitch, when they almost missed a depot near the Devil's Glacier, up on the polar plateau.

That glacier, this time, gave them no trouble at all, and they missed the Devil's Ballroom completely. The descent of the Axel Heiberg Glacier, on the other hand, turned into a memorable ski run.

Down from the plateau, Amundsen had raced for home. With a well marked route, he did sometimes 50 miles a day.

Another view of Framheim (*right*), with the Norwegian flag flying to show that Amundsen was back from the Pole.

No pictures have survived from the return journey. Amundsen simply raced along. When he reached Framheim, he had been out for ninety-nine days, and covered 1340 nautical miles. "We have far too many biscuits," he had written around 83°S, "and can do no better than give them to the dogs. They are putting on weight every day;" which was true of the men as well.

*Fram* had brought Amundsen news from the outside world.

A number of people seem to be indignant over our activities down here [Amundsen noted in his diary] – breach of "etiquette"? Are these people mad? Is the question of the Pole exclusively confined to Scott for solution? . . . Oh well, people are idiotic.

Thus Amundsen learned of the reaction to his change of plan. He had, however, won the race; and that ought to relegate all argument to the category of sour grapes.

On the 30th January, Amundsen embarked on *Fram* for Hobart, Tasmania. With him, he had all his surviving dogs. It was, he wrote, as he sailed out of the Bay of Whales,

a heavy moment to leave Framheim. A more splendid or pleasanter winter quarters no one has had. When we departed, Lindstrøm had scoured it from top to bottom and it was shining like a new pin. We won't be accused of untidiness or dirt if anyone should happen to go there and look.

*Fram* arrived at Hobart on the 7th March 1912. Soon after, the whole expedition was photographed on deck. Standing, left to right: Hassel, Ludvig Hansen, Steller (joined at Buenos Aires), Bjaaland, Kristensen, Rønne, Beck, Wisting, Halvorsen (joined at Buenos Aires), Sundbeck. Seated, left to right: Johansen, Prestrud, Amundsen, Thorvald Nilsen, Gjertsen, Helmer Hanssen. In front, left to right: Lindstrøm, Stubberud, Karenius Olsen and A. Olsen (joined at Buenos Aires).

Until the newspaper with which Amundsen's brother Leon had negotiated a contract published his news, he had to keep it secret. When he arrived at Hobart, he did not even know which newspaper it was to be. *Fram* refused to identify herself when she entered the harbour. She anchored out in the fairway, incommunicado. Amundsen went ashore alone and, as he noted in his diary:

> got a room at the Orient Hotel – Treated as a tramp – my peaked cap and blue sweater – given a miserable little room . . . Visited the Consul . . . Then I cabled to the King . . . Nansen and Leon. The day passed quietly, except for reporters, who were insistent, but without result.

The next day, Amundsen

> received a telegram from Leon, instructing me to cable my report to The Daily Chronicle, London. This was immediately done. After that, I kept very quiet. When I had gone to bed – 10 p.m. – the telegrams began to rain down – the King's came first . . .

# III

# *THE MAUD EXPEDITION*

1918–1923

ALASKA

Bering Strait

East Cape

Cape Serdze Kamen

Chukchee Peninsula

North Cape

Ayon Island

Pansileika

Kolyma River

Tsar Nicholas II Land
[Bolshevik Island]

Maud Haven

NORWAY

Vadsø

Novaya
Zemlya

Yugor Strait

Dickson Island

Cape
Chelyuskin

Khabarova

Yenisei River

R U S S I A

SIBERIA

# THE MAUD
# EXPEDITION

After winning the race for the South Pole, Amundsen gathered his lantern slides, and started out on the lecture trail once more. Having landed in Tasmania, he first toured Australia and New Zealand. Then he went to Buenos Aires. There, for the first time, he met Don Pedro Christopherson, his expatriate fellow-countryman, providential benefactor. During the autumn of 1912, Amundsen lectured on the Continent and in England, finally, in January 1913, going to the United States.

So far – with the exception of some chagrin in England – Amundsen had enjoyed universal acclaim. In February 1913, Scott's expediton finally returned, bringing confirmation of Amundsen's staggering victory and technical superiority. As he had put it, Scott was indeed "the first to visit the place after us". Unfortunately, Scott and all his companions had perished on the return. No matter that it was demonstrably his own ineptitude; the disaster was a sensation greater than the elegant solution that Amundsen achieved. In England, incompetence was concealed, and national pride salved by elevating the perpetrator to posthumous hero. One way or another, Amundsen found himself eclipsed.

He had publicly called his descent on the South Pole an "extension" of his original Arctic drift. On returning from Antarctica in 1912, he resumed his preparations. Questions of honour aside, there was little choice. Amundsen had no profession; polar exploration was his calling.

Although with Don Pedro's help, Amundsen paid most of his debts, money remained a stumbling block. Waiting in Buenos Aires, *Fram*'s timbers were found to be rotting. She returned to Norway in July 1914, as the First World War broke out. Amundsen still did not give up hope. Norway remained neutral; her merchant ships were in demand among the Allies. Like many of his countrymen, Amundsen invested in shipping. Guided by his brother, Leon, he was soon able to sell out with a profit of about 1,000,000 *kroner*.

That seemed enough to finance a new expedition or, as Amundsen still considered it, the resumption of the old one. The war had now lasted for a year and a half and, in Amundsen's own words,

I had no guarantee that it would not last much, much longer. If I were to wait until it finished, I felt that I could throw away the best years of my life, and that did not fit in with my plans. Another thing I had realized was that prices, which were already disturbingly high, would rise with phenomenal speed and make the enterprise impossible, even if I quintupled my capital. So: Keep going, and head for the goal for the 5th time!

*Fram* was laid up, unseaworthy, and uneconomic to repair. In 1916, Amundsen ordered a new wooden vessel. His fears were amply confirmed. Suppliers held the shipyard to ransom over timber and other material, all of which was in short supply. The final cost made a mockery of all allowance for wartime inflation.

In June 1917, however, the ship was finally launched. Amundsen called her *Maud*, after the Queen of Norway. Like *Fram*, she was designed to be frozen into the arctic pack ice, and lift under pressure to avoid being crushed. Amundsen, however, wished to improve on *Fram*'s lines, and had *Maud* constructed like an egg under the waterline.

Meanwhile, Amundsen was hindered in obtaining supplies. Because the Norwegian Government had taken no precautions, and refused to introduce rationing, there was a food shortage. Despite the war at sea, Amundsen visited America to order provisions. The United States was still neutral, but, before Amundsen's orders were delivered, had entered the war. All exports were stopped. Somehow, he obtained an export licence, and everything arrived in time.

On 24th June 1918 Amundsen left Christiania in *Maud*, eight years almost to the day after he had sailed on *Fram* for the south. There was some danger from German submarines, but Admiral Sims, of the U.S. Navy, had given Amundsen advice on time and route to minimize the danger. In any case, no submarines were sighted.

As he had originally intended, Amundsen was heading for the Bering Strait, to find a current that supposedly flowed northwards across the Arctic basic. On *Fram*, however, he was to sail via Horn and the coast of America. Now, on *Maud*, he was going through the North East Passage, along the coast of Siberia. On the 18th July 1918, *Maud* left Vardø, in northern Norway, and headed eastwards over the Barents Sea.

Amundsen had hoped to get all the way to the Bering Strait in one season. On the 17th September 1918, *Maud* was brought up by ice off Cape Chelyuskin, and frozen in for the winter. On the 10th February 1919, Amundsen wrote:

> Today I begin my story of the *Maud* Expedition – not with events fresh in my memory, but with events swiftly unfolding – Not as a victor who, in his publicity can afford to draw a shining veil over the reverse side of the medal & only allow the polished front to be seen; but with the long, long road towards the goal ahead of us . . . I . . . will do my best to report whatever happens, as it appears to me.

In fact, Amundsen had just suffered his first real setback as leader of a polar expedition. On the other hand he was the first explorer to winter at Cape Chelyuskin, and one of the last westerners to see this part of Siberia.

Cape Chelyuskin is the northernmost point of the old world. Across the water, over the ice, lay recently discovered territory, then called Tsar Nicholas II Land; but now known as Bolshevik Island. Amundsen had sailed after the Bolshevik revolution, and Russia was in turmoil. The Bolsheviks, however, were not yet secure in the saddle, and their power did not then extend to Siberia. When it did, Siberia was closed to outsiders.

*Maud* lay in a shallow bight, about 20 miles east of Cape Chelyuskin. Her anchorage was called Maudhaven, like Gjøahaven on the North West Passage. With him, Amundsen had Helmer Hanssen, who had been there too. He also had Oscar Wisting; so three of the five men who had reached the South Pole were now gathered in Siberia. Knut Sundbeck, *Fram*'s chief engineer, had the same berth on *Maud*. Martin Rønne, *Fram*'s sailmaker, was also on board. The expedition had five other members, including Dr Harald Ulrik Sverdrup, a Norwegian oceanographer, subsequently Director of the Scripps-Howard Oceanographic Institute at La Jolla, California.

"This winter was most monotonous," as Helmer Hanssen put it. "We had nothing to do except wait for the ice to release us, so that we could start on [the Arctic drift]." In April and May 1919, Amundsen sent three parties out to explore the environs of Cape Chelyuskin. He himself remained on the ship. His luck was out.

During the winter, Amundsen first of all broke his arm. Then he was mauled by a polar bear. Early in December 1918, he suffered from carbon monoxide poisoning when working in an unventilated magnetic observatory illuminated by a faulty paraffin lamp. He took a long time to recover, his heart was permanently strained, and for the next few years, he went on no long sledge journeys.

On the 16th August after a cold summer with persistent ice, *Maud* finally broke out of her winter quarters. Only on the 12th September, did the ice open and allow her to continue on her way. She left two of her crew behind at Cape Chelyuskin.

During the winter, a sailor called Peter Tessem had complained of persistent headaches. In any case, he clearly wanted to leave the expedition. Amundsen decided to send him home, and asked for someone to accompany him. Significantly the whole crew volunteered; with the sole exception of Sverdrup. Amundsen chose a sailor called Paul Knutsen. They were to travel overland by dog sledge to Dickson Island, at the mouth of the Yenisei River, whence they would return home to Norway. Both had been on expeditions to Siberia before. The journey was about 400 miles over easy terrain, and considered well within their capabilities. They never got through.

Meanwhile, on the 23rd September *Maud* was stopped by ice again. She was frozen in for a second winter on the Siberian coast, 500 miles short of the Bering Strait. She lay off Anyon Island, near the mouth of the Kolyma River.

At Cape Chelyuskin, Amundsen had been completely isolated from human contact. It was like the Antarctic all over again, without the inspiration of an incomparable prize ahead. At Anyon Island, circumstances were different. There was an encampment of Chukchees ashore. They were the first fresh faces for a year, and thenceforth the expedition had intermittent company.

The Chukchees were one of the least known of the eastern Siberian tribes. They were comparatively isolated; their contact with their Russian overlords was minimal. They were reindeer nomads, speaking a language of their own. Since *Maud* was stuck for six months at least, Amundsen decided that the Chukchees ought to be investigated. He did not wish to leave the ship, and suggested to Sverdrup that he follow the Chukchees on their migration into the interior, and study their customs.

Sverdrup enthusiastically agreed. Although a physicist by training, he felt that anthropology was well within his capability, and why not? He spent seven and a half months with the Chukchees during 1919–1920. He learned the language, produced a book on his work, and took a series of magnetic observations into the bargain.

On *Maud*, meanwhile, Amundsen was in dead water, his Arctic drift seemingly as far off as ever. At least he was in the polar regions, and not eating his heart out in civilization. Because of the delay, however, it was imperative that he make contact with home. Again, he did not feel able to leave the ship. For one thing, his heart had still not recovered from the carbon monoxide poisoning of the winter before. Since he had no doctor on board, he had no way of discovering what exactly ailed him.

At all events, in December 1919, Amundsen sent Helmer Hanssen and Wisting on a journey with dogs and sledge to find a cable station and communicate with Norway. With them was Tønnesen, one of *Maud*'s seamen, who now wanted to go home.

Tønnesen was by nature quiet and slow of speech. He had now reached a point where he demanded absolute silence while he worked. If anyone dared to speak, he lost his temper. It was clearly time for him to go. He turned out to be troublesome on the journey. Hanssen and Wisting left him at North Cape, about 150 miles to the east of *Maud*. There, a Russian trader promised to send him home.

Amundsen had told Hanssen and Wisting to go to Nome, in Alaska. When they reached the Bering Strait, however, the ice was uncertain, and dangerous to cross on foot. Nor were any ferries sailing. It was now February 1920. The Bolsheviks were approaching this corner of Siberia, and the place was in the vacuum between one régime and the other.

Leaving Wisting at East Cape, on the Bering Strait, Hanssen went on alone southwards to Anadyr, on the Bering Sea, in the hope that the telegraph station there was in operation. He took care to leave all papers behind that might brand him as a spy. When he reached Anadyr, on the 23rd March, he observed the town full of red flags.

America and the Bolshevik régime were then in the twilight world between peace and war. In any case they had no diplomatic relations and, officially, there was no communication over the Bering Strait. Nonetheless, the Russian radio station at Anadyr managed to make contact with the American one at St Paul. Amundsen's name was its own passport.

Having received a reply to his telegram, Helmer Hanssen started on the return journey. He picked up Wisting at East Cape in May, and on the 14th June 1920 they were back on *Maud*. Hanssen had travelled by dog sledge 1,000 miles, and spent over six months to send a few telegrams.

Amundsen now changed his plans. Instead of starting the polar drift when he could get clear of his winter quarters, and enter the main pack ice, he decided first to sail to Nome, and refit. At that, Helmer Hanssen, Sundbeck and Rønne decided to leave the expedition. This they did, at Nome, when *Maud* arrived there on the 27th July 1920. Amundsen had thereby completed the North East Passage.

Ten days later, Amundsen sailed again. There were now exactly four men on board, to work a three masted auxiliary schooner of 400 tons, and sustain a drift of up to five years. Fortunately, perhaps, this third attempt failed too. The Bering Strait was full of ice, and *Maud* was stopped at Cape Serdze Kamen, on the Siberian side, a bare seventy miles to the west. There, she spent her third winter in the ice.

At the end of January, Sverdrup and Wisting left the ship with two dog teams to follow the coast of the Chukchee Peninsula to Holy Cross Bay. Although the Bolsheviks had now taken over, the curtain had not yet come down, and access was still relatively easy. Sverdrup and Wisting were back in May, having covered 1,200 miles. Blizzards kept them weather-bound for twenty-three days.

On 1st July 1921, *Maud* was able to break out of the ice, and leave her winter quarters. It was three years since she had started on her voyage, and still had not started on her drift. There was no question of doing so now. Her propeller was damaged, and she required other repairs. Reluctantly or not, Amundsen headed back through the Bering Strait, and on the 31st August *Maud* tied up at Seattle, Washington, where she was overhauled. Amundsen then went back to Norway to look after his affairs.

He returned to *Maud* in June 1922, at Nome. Now he had with him an aeroplane, in which he hoped to fly across the Arctic. He took it on board, and a few weeks later transshipped, with it, to an Alaskan schooner to go to Wainwright. He then left the expedition.

*Maud*, meanwhile, refitted and with a fresh crew, continued under Wisting's command. He tried to start the Arctic drift as originally planned, but somehow could not find the expected northerly current. *Maud* got no further than the New Siberian Islands. At least, she survived unscathed in the ice-covered polar sea, which had crushed other ships. Wisting extricated her from the pack ice, and brought her back to Nome on 22nd August 1925.

There, she was impounded for debts unpaid since her previous visits. She was released with the help of some Norwegians living in Nome and, after a stormy passage, reached Seattle. There, she was impounded once more. Amundsen had not managed to fly across the Arctic, and had declared himself bankrupt.

*Maud* was sold to the Hudson's Bay Company, and eventually foundered off Victoria Island, in the Canadian Arctic.

Although on *Maud*, Amundsen had become the second man to sail through the North East Passage, he regarded the expedition as a failure. At least, it had given him more lantern slides to add to his collection. With these in his baggage, he set out to earn money, if he could, and return to the polar regions.

*Maud* in her first winter quarters, near Cape Chelyuskin, the northernmost point of the Eurasian land mass. This picture was taken in the spring of 1919.

Amundsen was one of the last westerners to see the place. Soon afterwards, the Bolshevik régime extended its sway to the whole of Siberia, and the Arctic coast was closed to outsiders.

The dogs and sledge in this picture belong to a party returning from a traverse of Cape Chelyuskin. As far as Amundsen knew, he was the first explorer to winter there; and the first perhaps to survey the interior. Many features were yet unnamed, and one he called Mount Fridtjof Nansen. He had given the same name to another mountain, at the other end of the world, on the way to the South Pole.

Another view of *Maud* in her winter quarters off Cape Chelyuskin. The stack of firewood in the background came from driftwood, of which there is much along the Siberian Arctic coast. It is carried down the great rivers flowing through the forests of the interior.

The figure in the foreground, festooned with fish and game he had caught, is Gennady Olonkin. He was a Russian who joined the expedition, on an impulse, at Khabarova, on the Yugor Strait, near Novaya Zemlya.

Olonkin was a telegraphist, and happened to speak Norwegian. As Amundsen noted, he was

scarcely 21 years old . . . It has always been my opinion that anyone who joined an expedition of this type ought to be at least 30. But I had to admit that here I was faced with an exception. Unless I was seriously mistaken, he would yield to no one in the way he did his duty. We needed an extra hand on board, and undoubtedly could make use of him. He said he could sign on as 2nd Engineer, and that was exactly what was needed.

Rønne and Sundbeck collecting driftwood at Maudhaven,
Cape Chelyuskin, winter 1918–19.

On the 16th August 1919, *Maud* left her winter quarters at Cape Chelyuskin; by the 23rd September, she was brought up by ice again, and had to spend a second winter beset on the Siberian coast. She had sailed about 3,000 miles since leaving Norway, and was still 500 miles short of the Bering Strait, where she was supposed to begin her drift across the Arctic. After more than a year, Amundsen had not even started his real enterprise.

He now wanted to make contact with the outside world.

*Maud* did have a radio, but it could not receive anything; and there was no guarantee that its transmissions were being picked up. Amundsen decided to send a party with post to Nishny Kolymsk, the nearest town, on the Kolyma River, about 200 miles inland. He chose Helmer Hanssen, Wisting and Olonkin.

This picture shows them leaving *Maud* on the 20th October 1919. The objects on the rigging are furs hung out to dry.

Amundsen and Olonkin, shovelling snow off the deck of *Maud* during the spring of 1919. She was still at Cape Chelyuskin.

Amundsen was in contact with Russians and various Siberian tribesmen travelling along the coast. From them, he understood that the Bolsheviks were now extending their grip to Siberia. In his own words, he told Olonkin that

as soon as he arrives at Nishny Kolymsk, he is to report to the highest authorities, say that we are lying here, and that we have been bartering with the natives for our own use. I am not sure that we will not have unpleasantness in the spring.

Gennady Olonkin, the Russian who joined *Maud* at Khabarova. Now that he was stuck on the Siberian coast, Amundsen was glad of an interpreter. Neither he nor his companions spoke Russian.

Olonkin spoke Norwegian well. He probably learned the language through contact with the Norwegians running the Siberian Trading Company. This had been formed before the war to promote trade between Siberia and the West. It owned ships plying up the Yenisei River into the interior.

Oscar Wisting on *Maud*. He had been at the South Pole with Amundsen.

On the 1st December 1919 Wisting left *Maud* on a journey, with dogs and sledge, that took six months. *Maud* was then frozen in off Ayon Island. Helmer Hanssen, Olonkin and Tønnesen had failed to get through with the post. Amundsen then asked Wisting, together with Helmer Hanssen, to go to Nome, in Alaska, with post and telegrams.

That meant crossing the Bering Strait, which turned out to be impossible. The ice was unsafe to cross on foot, and no ships were running. So the telegrams had to be sent from Anadyr, on the Siberian side of the Bering Sea. Hanssen and Wisting returned to *Maud* on the 14th June 1920, with replies to their telegrams. They had travelled about 1,000 miles.

Wisting described how, on the way out, they reached North Cape, where

we had confirmation of news we had already heard: The World War had finished in the autumn of 1918, and there had been great upheavals in Europe. Better late than never – we heard this news about one and a half years after the events had taken place.

Peter Tessem, on the deck of *Maud* (*left*) and in the saloon
(*right*). During the first winter, he had complained of a
constant headache. Amundsen decided to send him home,
taking post and scientific results. On the 12th September
1919, while *Maud* was still stuck in the ice thirty-six miles
to the east of Cape Chelyushkin, he left with ski, dogs and
sledge, for Dickson Island, the first stage on his journey
back to Norway. Although it was 400 miles to Dickson
Island, the route was overland through easy terrain, with
occasional settlements, and thought to be well within the
capabilities of a seasoned Arctic traveller like Tessem.

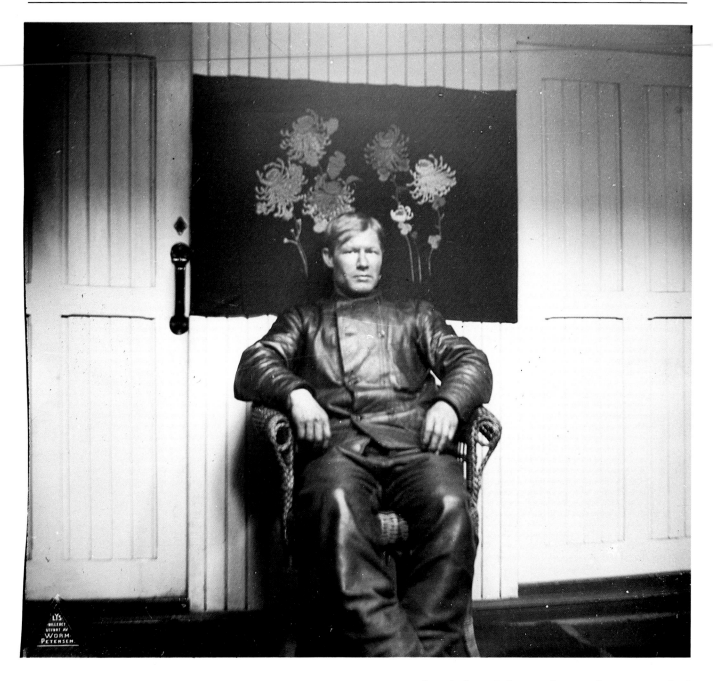

Paul Knutsen, who accompanied Tessem on his journey home. They vanished somewhere along the Siberian coast, and were never seen alive again. A skeleton was later found within sight of Dickson Island, and believed to be that of either Tessem or Knutsen. The cause of their disappearance remains a mystery.

When Tessem and Knutsen left *Maud*, only eight men remained on board. "I have had to give up my cherished plan of leaving the ship and attaining the Pole with dogs and sledges," Amundsen then wrote. "Our experience has shown that we cannot work the ship with fewer than 8 hands."

Amundsen believed that neither Cook nor Peary had actually reached the North Pole, and wanted to be the first man at *both* poles of the earth.

*Right*] Dr Harald Ulrik Sverdrup in *Maud*'s saloon. *Maud*'s winter quarters in 1919–20, at Ayon Island, lay in territory inhabited by a remote Siberian tribe called the Chukchees.

Amundsen sent Sverdrup to live with the Chukchees for six months, and write an anthropological report. Although Sverdrup was trained as a physicist, he had a great interest in human nature, and did this work well. It produced the one lasting result of the expedition. Of him, Amundsen wrote that

> one might form the false impression that Sverdrup is a boring scientist . . . Nothing could be more misleading . . . he is the world's most natural person, cheerful, free of all affectation, often a sheer schoolboy in his behaviour.

Sverdrup, for his part, was taken aback by Amundsen's sensitivity:

If in conversation Amundsen would make a statement which to the best of my knowledge was incorrect, I would draw his attention to [the] mistake . . . One day . . . Amundsen flared up: "Why do you always contradict . . . me? Because you have a degree you seem to think that you have all knowledge and experience . . . You are breaking down morale . . . you are making me appear ridiculous . . . You will have to leave the expedition . . . You will get what equipment you need and you go!"

For a week he did not speak to me. [Then] I went to him. "I have never intended to hurt you . . . in the future . . . I shall keep my opinions to myself until asked for and I shall avoid what may appear as unnecessary criticism." . . . We shook hands.

The incident was never referred to again.

Rønne at the door of his cabin on *Maud*. Amundsen wrote of him that he

> holds the odd record of being the expedition's oldest youngest member. By that I mean that in years he is the oldest, but in spirit younger than the youngest of us. I have never seen him otherwise than cheerful. Always ready for a joke, even if it is against him. Never takes offence. If I am bored, I merely have to wind him up, and an endless succession of stories from all corners of the earth is unrolled for me. Rønne has blue blood, fine hands and descent. His family tree hangs framed above his bunk. But it only goes back to the 12th Century, in other words, parvenus. If one discusses the matter with him – and he is not at all unwilling – even Odin and Tor may be glimpsed in the distance! . . . He is really a sailmaker, but I can also give him the very finest reference as shoemaker, tailor, saddlemaker, furrier and bookbinder. If one adds his great talent as model maker, I think it is unnecessary to mention any more of his many other qualities to understand that he is capable, and indispensable on an expedition such as this.

Helmer Hanssen (left) and Wisting in *Maud*'s saloon, after their return on the 14th June 1920, from their long journey to the Bering Sea.

With them, they had taken a sailor called Tønnesen, who wanted to leave the expedition. They left him at North Cape, on the outward journey, where a Russian merchant promised to send him home to Norway.

Soon after this picture was taken, Helmer Hanssen also decided to leave the expedition. However, he agreed to . stay until *Maud* reached Nome, where Amundsen had now decided to take her. There, he wanted to replenish his supplies before starting on his polar drift. Wisting, on the other hand, wanted to remain with Amundsen.

Sverdrup in the laboratory on *Maud*.

Helmer Hanssen in his cabin on *Maud*. Besides himself, Sundbeck, the chief engineer, and Rønne had decided to leave the expedition on reaching Nome.

Knutsen in the galley on *Maud*. Originally, Lindstrøm was to have been cook, but fell ill shortly before departure, and could not sail. After Knutsen left the expedition in September 1919, there was no regular cook, and some of the eight remaining members took turns.

Amundsen was one. He was adjudged a very good cook. Sverdrup, who also served in the galley, praised Amundsen's baking highly. He was singularly adept at puff pastry.

Sundbeck's workshop, in a corner of the engine room, on *Maud*. Like *Fram*, she had a diesel motor. Sundbeck and Rønne, Amundsen wrote,

must really be mentioned simultaneously, since they are inseparable. It is no disparagement to say that Rønne likes a little chat, and Sundbeck has the special quality of always appearing to listen with interest. He is without equal in that respect. When Rønne tells a story for the 20th time, the rest of us shout: "We've heard that one before!" But not Sundbeck. He thinks the 20th time is just as interesting as the first, and naturally the consequence is that Rønne always seeks his company, and always has something to say, even if it is not new.

Amundsen said that *Maud's*

crowning glory was the engine room . . . Sundbeck managed to arrange a control centre down there, from which he controlled the whole ship. He could do the most unbelievable things just by pressing a button. A network of pipes was gathered here, so that he could have everything he needed – diesel oil, lubricating oil, etc. In my enthusiasm, when I first saw it all . . . I asked Sundbeck if he couldn't turn a tap, and give me an ale? "No," he answered smiling faintly, "but you can always have a lager."

A corner of the saloon on *Maud*.

Amundsen in the saloon on *Maud*. His large, aquiline nose
was a cartoonist's delight.

Sundbeck's tidal gauge. He had arranged it so that the dial could be read on *Maud's* deck. It is under the winter awning, which ran the length of the ship. Some snow has nonetheless made its way inside.

One of the kites used by Sverdrup for meteorological observations. "I still feel the old schoolboy excitement at seeing a kite rise," Amundsen wrote. "And think of all the strange information it brings down!"

Easter 1919: Sundbeck and Rønne on Godfred Hansen's Islands. This was a group of islets in *Maud*'s winter harbour near Cape Chelyushkin. Amundsen named some of the features he surveyed after members of the North West Passage expedition.

That same year, Godfred Hansen, in Denmark, was preparing to lead what he called "The Third Thule Expedition". This went via Thule, in northern Greenland, to Cape Columbia, the tip of North America. There, Hansen put out a depot for Amundsen, in case he reached the North Pole by sledge, as he had intended, and retreated via the American coast.

Helmer Hanssen and Wisting scraping the fat off the pelt of a polar bear. In the course of the expedition several were shot. During the first winter, Amundsen was mauled by a polar bear. He told the story in these words:

The morning was so fine, that I went for a walk on the ice . . . Out of the subdued light . . . I saw Jakob [one of the dogs] speeding along like an arrow, followed by a bear. When the bear noticed me, he stopped, sat on his hind legs, with fore paws held up, and looked at me . . . Like a rocket I tore off towards . . . the gangway – screaming Bear! Bear! . . . I must have managed a phenomenal speed, because I reached the gangway . . . and that was the end . . . I heard a horrible roar in my ear, and the next moment, I was laid flat on the gangway with a well-placed blow. "What did you think of when you lay under the bear, grandad," my grandchildren will almost certainly ask. "Well, my children," I will answer, "in a second or two, you will have a bear's tooth in your neck." What saved me was that I lay absolutely still [and then] Jakob's reappearance. As I waited to be dispatched, I noticed a movement that made me turn my head. At that moment, the bear jumped . . . Like lightning, I was on my feet, up the gangway, and on the deck.

Wisting eventually shot the bear.

In spite of all, Amundsen was well disposed to most
animals, including polar bears. He caught a bear cub,
which he called Marie, and tried to tame her. To begin
with, she was obliging. Here she is taking Sverdrup's cap
off.

– And here she is running away with it. One day, Amundsen had to record in his diary that he

put Marie down with chloroform. I had given up hope of training her. After I had cared for her and fed her for a month, she . . . went for me in a fury. Under the care of an experienced animal trainer, perhaps she could have learned to behave herself, but I had to give up.

Russians alongside *Maud*, off Ayon Island, where she was frozen in for the second time in her voyage through the North East Passage along the Siberian coast.

This picture was taken during the spring of 1920. The Bolsheviks were approaching north eastern Siberia, but while Amundsen was there, it was still no man's land. He reported some of his visitors saying that they preferred the Tsar, because then they had tobacco and vodka, and now they had neither.

When the Bolsheviks took over, this region was closed to outsiders. *Maud* was lying near the Kolyma river, the surroundings of which later held some of the sinister concentration camps of the new régime. It is the original Gulag. Amundsen and his companions were among the last Westerners to visit the place; voluntarily at any rate.

The bell on a half finished Russian church at Pansileika.

While *Maud* lay off Ayon Island, Harald Sverdrup followed Chukchee tribesmen into the interior, and lived with them for six months. They numbered a few thousand, and although they had contact with Russian traders, Sverdrup appeared to have been the first European to spend a winter with them.

Sverdrup took this picture at the annual market at Pansileika. This was a Russian settlement on a tributary of the Kolyma River.

At Pansileika, the Chukchees bartered with Russian traders. They had chiefly reindeer, which they exchanged for civilized wants. This picture shows a herd of reindeer brought to market. Sverdrup described how trading took place:

> The Russian traders stood in their stalls . . . The stall was unfurnished, but against the back wall was a platform on which the trader stood . . . Business took place without many words.

The Chukchee came in and delivered . . . what he had. "What do you need?" the trader would ask, and according to the reply, he would give the Chukchee tea, tobacco, matches, knives, or cartridges, without anything more being said. Most of the Russian traders, incidentally, speak excellent Chukchee; some of them as well as the natives.

Sverdrup observed that the Chukchees

settled their minor disagreements in the most primitive way; by fighting, but under the Russians, the fighting now rarely involved drawing blood . . . Here the law of the fist is supreme. A man called Oærive bought a rifle and cartridges from . . . Oomye; that is to say he had received the gun and cartridges, but there was no agreement on price, or when payment should take place. A year later, Oomye thought it was time to visit Oærive and demand payment, but added that if Oærive could avoid paying, he would, so they would undoubtedly have to fight. "Fight?" I asked, "You must surely be paid for your gun even if he beats you?" "No," he replied. "If Oærive manages to beat me, I will not be paid."

Pansileika market: an old Chukchee woman being persuaded by a Russian trader to allow Sverdrup to photograph her.

Sverdrup was mystified by Chukchee family relationships until, as he said he "learned of a relationship which explained everything".

When two Chukchees are good friends, they exchange wives. When they visit each other, they sleep with each others' wives . . . In this way, double alliances occur, in which each man has two wives, and each woman two husbands. Triple alliances also exist, but in that case, two of the men must not be brothers . . . A man in one of these double marriages not only calls his wife's children his own, but also those of his friend; but when the wives go so far as to call another wife's children hers, it becomes a motley; also when the children all call each other brothers and sisters.

A Chukchee encampment at East Cape, during Wisting's
stay. The lady facing the camera has evidently absorbed
European ways.

Chukchees from East Cape, on the Russian side of the Bering Strait, visiting *Maud* at Ayon Island. It was on their trading route along the North Coast of Siberia. On the 5th December 1919, Amundsen noted in his diary that he

had to make the Chukchees understand that the saloon is not for them. I have not the slightest inclination to have 13 people, some of whom are full of lice, in here the whole day, and cook food for them into the bargain. I sent some tinned food to them on land.

Amundsen considered that "the coastal population of Northern Siberia is at a very low state of development."

I have no hesitation in saying that they are considerably beneath the Eskimos on the Alaskan coast. But they have continual contact with the outside world. Sundbeck showed a film . . . to [the Chukchees] – you should have seen these children of Nature! When people began to dance on the screen, their amazement knew no bounds.

When Helmer Hanssen and Wisting travelled across the Chukchee Peninsula to send Amundsen's telegrams, they separated at East Cape, on the Bering Strait. Hanssen went on alone to Anadyr, where there was a telegraph station. Wisting waited behind at East Cape.

There he stayed with an Australian trader called Charles Carpendale, who was married to a native woman, probably a Chukchee. This picture shows Carpendale (*right*) in his home. The figure on the left may be that of the last Tsarist Governor of the district. Not long after Wisting left, the Bolsheviks arrived, and the Governor fled to Alaska.

Before the Bolshevik revolution, there was free traffic

across the Bering Strait. Disappointed gold diggers from Alaska sometimes tried their luck on the Russian side. In consequence, there was a cosmopolitan sprinkling along the coast. During their journey, Hanssen and Wisting met some Norwegians, a Dutchman and a Pole, besides the usual Russian traders.

Wisting stayed with Carpendale from the 1st February until 18th May 1920. By then, Helmer Hanssen finally returned from Anadyr, and they started on the journey back to *Maud.*

A Chukchee sacrificial mound of reindeer antlers on Ayon Island, near *Maud's* winter harbour.

The Chukchees were nomads, following the reindeer in their migration. The reindeer consequently dominated their life.

The religion of the Chukchees was a form of shamanism. They believed in good and evil spirits; fearing the one rather more than they worshipped the other. Sacrificial mounds of this kind usually were intended to propitiate evil spirits.

Rønne at Ayon Island holding mammoth tusks presented to Amundsen by a Russian trader. Siberia is the home of the mammoth and, in those days, mammoth ivory was in great demand. Before the advent of plastic, it was much used for billiard balls and expensive hair brushes.

The magnetic observatory next to *Maud* at Ayon Island. The study of terrestrial magnetism was one of the objects of the expedition. Very few observations had yet been made in this region.

The object was to measure the intensity and fluctuation of the earth's magnetic field. Also, Sverdrup tried to photograph the aurora borealis, but was only partially successful.

Amundsen reading the magnetometer in the magnetic observatory. He is determining the horizontal component of the earth's magnetic field. He never claimed to be a scientist, but was interested in terrestrial magnetism. This originated on the *Belgica*, twenty years before, when one of the aims of the expedition had been the location of the South Magnetic Pole.

Before the days of the gyro compass, satellites, and radio navigation, the magnetic compass remained the only directional instrument. For that reason, a precise knowledge of the earth's magnetic field, and hence compass error, was vital.

In the summer of 1920, *Maud* reached Nome, Alaska. Amundsen had taken a ship from the Atlantic, along the Siberian coast, through the Bering Strait, and into the approaches to the Pacific. He had completed the North East Passage; the second man in recorded history to do so. The first was the Swede, Baron A. E. Nordenskiöld, in the *Vega* in 1878–79.

Nonetheless, Amundsen had still not entered the Arctic drift, which was the real purpose of his expedition. On the 8th August 1920, after reprovisioning, he left Nome to try once more. *Maud* was brought up by the ice at Cape Serdze Kamen in Siberia, on the northern approaches to the Bering Strait. There, she was frozen in for yet another winter.

At Cape Serdze Kamen, *Maud* had what Amundsen considered a stream of visitors all through the winter and into the summer of 1921. Here are two of them.

Although this part of Siberia was Chukchee territory the woman on the right appears to have Eskimo blood.

Two more visitors to *Maud* at Cape Serdze Kamen.

Two more visitors to *Maud* at Cape Serdze Kamen, photographed under the winter awning. "The whole winter we had as neighbours three Chukchee tents," Amundsen wrote. "We naturally became good friends."

Otherwise I would not have dared to question the most interesting of the families. It consisted of an old man, an old woman, and a boy of six. One day I asked the woman "Is that your son?" . . . To my surprise, she answered simply "Yes." She must have read the surprise in my face, for she added, "My husband got him." Then she told me the whole story. She said that although they had married while very young . . .

they had been childless until both were quite old and it was quite certain that they would never have any children. It was a great disappointment for both, so one day the wife said to her husband: "Let us not grow old without children in the house. So and so," and here she mentioned the name of another member of the tribe, "has a very pretty wife. Go and tell them how we would so very much like to have children and see if he would not allow her to bear one for us."

The man did as his wife asked him, and his helpful friend agreed. The result was the six year old boy I had asked about. While he was his father's biological son, he was just as much the mother's by virtue of the love which had caused his being.

Yet other visitors to *Maud* at Cape Serdze Kamen.

Chukchee visitors on the winter awning of *Maud* at Cape Serdze Kamen. In the Arctic, the sun also shines.

In 1921, *Maud* left Cape Serdze Kamen, and sailed to Seattle to refit. The following year she tried yet again to start on her Arctic drift. She got no further than the New Siberian Islands, and had to turn back. It was the end of a failed venture, and Amundsen's first setback twenty years after first going into the ice. Nonetheless, as he put it:

When I anchored [at Nome] after sailing through the North East Passage, I succeeded in connecting it with my North West Passage of 1906, and thus for the first time completed a circumnavigation of the Arctic Ocean. In this age of records that might have some significance.

# EPILOGUE

Amundsen's attempt to fly across the Arctic from Alaska, after leaving *Maud*, ended in a crash before he started. Meanwhile, the Norwegian Government had given him a grant of 500,000 kroner. This would have cleared his debts, but it had been swallowed by the abortive flight instead.

By now Amundsen was in financial distress. He had declared himself bankrupt. Legal proceedings were dragging on in Norway and America. At the age of 52, he had to start all over again:

> An ambitious dream had taken hold of me; to fly from continent to continent across the Arctic . . . The Pole itself held no interest for me – Peary's brilliant deed in 1909 had destroyed its value for all subsequent explorers.

In 1924, Amundsen was back in America, on the lecture trail once more, trying to raise money for another flight. With him, as so often in the past, were his slides from the North West Passage and the South Pole. To them were now added a selection from the North East Passage (as he called his part of the *Maud* expedition). In the autumn, he found himself in New York, after a tour which, in his own words, had turned out to be "practically a fiasco".

The glory of the South Pole had faded. The lantern lecture was being supplanted by the cinema as a public entertainment. Amundsen's star was on the wane. He told the story of how, one day, he was sitting in his room at the Waldorf-Astoria Hotel in New York, going over his finances. The results were "not encouraging. I worked out that if nothing unforeseen occurred, I could be ready to start when I was 110 years old!"

> As I sat and brooded in my room, the telephone rang . . . a man's voice asked if I was in, and added: "I met you many years ago in France, during the war."

Amundsen, in fact, had been one of the prominent citizens of neutral countries invited to tour the Allied front.

> Hundreds have introduced themselves in this way [Amundsen said], only to waste my time with stupid gossip. But there was perhaps an even better reason than usual for my short, negative answer. I also had less than pleasant experiences of visits which brought writs . . . I was not at all inclined to meet casual acquaintances, whose only recommendation was "a meeting in France".
>
> The next thing that was said, made me listen with pleasure:

> "I am an amateur in polar exploration, but I am extremely interested. Perhaps I could obtain money for another expedition." I need scarcely say that I asked him to come up immediately.

The visitor was an American called Lincoln Ellsworth, the son of a millionaire, and heir to a fortune. He was trying to persuade his profoundly reluctant father to finance an Arctic expedition of his own. By chance, Ellsworth saw a newspaper paragraph reporting Amundsen's presence in New York, and that gave him the key. He introduced Amundsen and his father to each other. Ellsworth père was impressed. Unwilling to trust his son in the frozen wastes he was, after a little persuasion, prepared to trust the conqueror of the South Pole. The money was forthcoming.

Amundsen was able to buy two German all-metal Dornier Wal flying boats, among the first of their kind. In May 1925, he flew from Spitsbergen towards the North Pole. With him were Lincoln Ellsworth, three Norwegians and a German mechanic. It was a hasty and ill-conceived venture.

Just south of the 88th parallel, both machines were forced down on to the pack ice, and one was damaged. Amundsen persuaded his companions to level a runway on a large ice floe, and make an attempt to take off in the undamaged aircraft. In Ellsworth's words, Amundsen enforced

> an orderly routine – fixed hours for meals, for work and sleep, and for smoking and talking. He knew there was no quicker way to break men down under strain than to allow them to live haphazardly. An ordered existence, moreover, engendered confidence. This calm and unhurried way of doing things seemed to symbolize the ability of intelligence to overcome the inimical forces of nature.

After three weeks' work with wholly inadequate tools, Amundsen and his companions managed to build a runway on the ice just long enough for takeoff. After several failures the pilot, Hjalmar Riiser-Larsen, somehow got the plane into the air. A few hours later, they were back on Spitsbergen, having been given up for lost.

At the age of fifty-three, Amundsen had spectacularly returned to the centre of the stage. He had reached

87°77′N, the furthest north yet in the air. Whereas the *Maud* expedition had been regarded as a failure, dimming his reputation, his escape from the jaws of the Arctic was considered a triumph. After this new exploit, on his return to Norway, he was given a rapturous reception by his countrymen.

Meanwhile, Ellsworth came into his inheritance and gave $100,000 towards a trans polar flight by airship under Amundsen's command. After his experience, Amundsen had decided that the future of polar flying lay with lighter than air craft. He bought an airship in Italy. As pilot, he took Umberto Nobile, her designer, and a leading authority on airships. The flight mechanics were also Italian. The airship, however, flew the Norwegian flag, and was named *Norge* ("Norway"). Although Ellsworth was American, he willingly acquiesced. His attitude to Amundsen was one of hero worship, and the only reward he wanted was the privilege of going on an expedition with him.

On the 6th May 1926, the *Norge* stopped at Vadsø, in northern Norway, on her way from Rome to Kings Bay, on Spitsbergen. It was the anniversary of that visit which led to the discovery of the slides in this book.

The *Norge* left Kings Bay on the 11th May, reaching Teller, Alaska, two days later. Shortly before, Commander (later Admiral) Richard E. Byrd had flown to the Pole in an aeroplane, starting and finishing at Kings Bay. Amundsen was therefore not quite the first man to fly over the North Pole. On the other hand, he was the first to fly across the Arctic. Moreover, he and Wisting, who was also on the flight, became the first men to reach both the North and South Poles.

Amundsen was welcomed home with admiration yet more frenzied than the previous year, after his escape from the ice. Now, at the age of 54, ambition more or less satisfied, he retired from polar exploration, the only profession he had known.

He was not, however, a happy man. He was burdened by loneliness and disillusion. He never married. He was still in debt, pursued by creditors. It was not easy to shrug off. He fell out with his brother, Leon, who suspected him of mismanaging his finances. He quarrelled publicly with Nobile, whom he accused of claiming too much credit for the flight of the *Norge*. He became increasingly embittered. It was almost as if he was paying a price for having achieved virtually everything he had set out to do.

Despite recognition elsewhere, Amundsen was angered by neglect among the English who, he alleged in his autobiography,

> feel obliged to denigrate an explorer, merely because he is not a compatriot . . . I have felt the effect of this in many ways in connection with our conquest both of the North West Passage and the South Pole . . .
>
> The year after my journey to the pole, the son of a prominent Norwegian living in London came home to his father and protested against having learned at school that Scott was the discoverer of the South Pole. On investigation, the boy was proven right, and also it was common in other schools to ignore the Norwegian expedition.

At the end of May 1928, Amundsen came out of retirement. Nobile had returned to the Arctic, this time under Italian colours, and disappeared on a flight to the North Pole in an airship called *Italia*. Because he had a radio, he was soon located, and rescue attempts turned into a race to be the first to reach him. Amundsen entered that race.

By now, with the aid of faithful friends, he was practically solvent. Nonetheless he suffered the humiliation of begging yet again. He craved action once more. Through the intercession of a Norwegian businessman living in Paris, the French Government provided a flying boat complete with pilot and crew. On the 18th June 1928, it took off from Tromsø, in northern Norway, with Amundsen on board. It was never seen again. All her crew were lost. Amundsen had vanished into the polar sea which was his only true home on earth.

# *INDEX*